ASIA

EXPLORING GEOGRAPHY

| PHYSICAL FEATURES | POLITICAL DIVISIONS | RESOURCES | CULTURE |

6368

Exploring geography: Asia
(Middle/Upper primary)

Published by Prim-Ed Publishing 2013 under licence from Evan-Moor® Educational Publishers

Copyright© 2010 Evan-Moor® Educational Publishers

This version copyright© Prim-Ed Publishing 2013

ISBN 978-1-84654-663-1

PR– 6368

Titles in this series:
Beginning geography *(Lower/Middle primary)*
Exploring geography: Africa *(Middle/Upper primary)*
Exploring geography: Antarctica *(Middle/Upper primary)*
Exploring geography: Asia *(Middle/Upper primary)*
Exploring geography: Australia & Oceania *(Middle/Upper primary)*
Exploring geography: Europe *(Middle/Upper primary)*
Exploring geography: North America *(Middle/Upper primary)*
Exploring geography: South America *(Middle/Upper primary)*

This master may only be reproduced by the original purchaser for use with their class(es). The publisher prohibits the loaning or onselling of this master for the purposes of reproduction.

Copyright Notice

Blackline masters or copy masters are published and sold with a limited copyright. This copyright allows publishers to provide teachers and schools with a wide range of learning activities without copyright being breached. This limited copyright allows the purchaser to make sufficient copies for use within their own education institution. The copyright is not transferable, nor can it be onsold. Following these instructions is not essential but will ensure that you, as the purchaser, have evidence of legal ownership to the copyright if inspection occurs.

For your added protection in the case of copyright inspection, please complete the form below. Retain this form, the complete original document and the invoice or receipt as proof of purchase.

Name of Purchaser:

_____

Date of Purchase:

_____

Supplier:

_____

School Order# (if applicable):

_____

Signature of Purchaser:

_____

Internet websites

In some cases, websites or specific URLs may be recommended. While these are checked and rechecked at the time of publication, the publisher has no control over any subsequent changes which may be made to webpages. It is *strongly* recommended that the class teacher checks *all* URLs before allowing pupils to access them.

View all pages online   **Website:** www.prim-ed.com

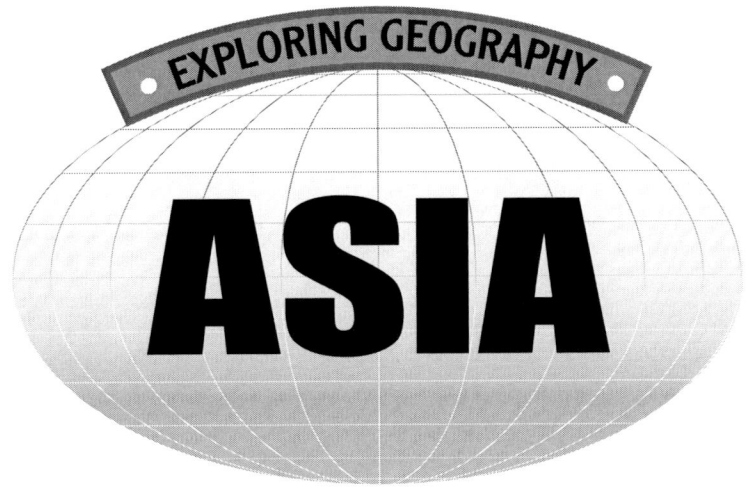

EXPLORING GEOGRAPHY
ASIA

CONTENTS

What's in this book 4

Section 1: Asia in the world 5–16

Section 2: Political divisions
ของ Asia. 17–42

Section 3: Physical features
of Asia. 43–68

Section 4: Valuable resources
of Asia 69–90

Section 5: Asian culture. 91–110

Section 6: Assessment 111–113

Section 7: Note-takers 114–120

Answers 121–126

CURRICULUM LINKS

COUNTRY	SUBJECT	LEVEL	OBJECTIVES
England	Geography	KS 2	• locate the world's countries, using maps, concentrating on their environmental regions, key physical and human characteristics, countries and major cities
			• identify the position and significance of latitude, longitude, Equator, Northern Hemisphere, Southern Hemisphere, the Tropics of Cancer and Capricorn, Arctic and Antarctic Circle, and the Prime/Greenwich Meridian
			• understand geographical similarities and differences through the study of human and physical geography
			• describe and understand key aspects of physical geography, including: climate zones, biomes and vegetation belts, rivers, mountains, volcanoes and earthquakes
			• describe and understand key aspects of human geography, including: types of settlement and land use, economic activity and the distribution of natural resources
			• use maps, atlases and globes to locate countries and describe features studied
			• use the eight points of a compass and symbols and key to build knowledge of the United Kingdom and the wider world

CURRICULUM LINKS

COUNTRY	SUBJECT	LEVEL	OBJECTIVES
Northern Ireland	The World Around Us	KS 1	• explore the interdependence of people and the environment • explore the effect of people on the natural environment over time • explore how place influences plant and animal life • explore features of the immediate world and comparisons between places • explore sources of energy in the world • study the life of a child in a contrasting location, including similarities and differences such as events and celebrations • compare the local area and a contrasting place; e.g. weather, landscape features
		KS 2	• explore the interdependence of people and the environment • explore the effect of people on the natural environment over time • explore how place influences the nature of life • explore features of, and variations in places, including physical, human, climatic, vegetation and animal life • know how we are interdependent with other parts of Europe and the wider world for some of our goods • compare places, such as location, size and resources • study weather in the local area compared to places that experience very different weather conditions • examine the effect of extreme weather conditions in the wider world, including the effect on places
Republic of Ireland	Geography	3rd/4th Class	• develop some awareness of the human and natural features of some places in other places in the world • establish and use cardinal compass points • develop familiarity with, and engage in practical use of maps • develop an understanding of and use some common map features and conventions • identify major geographical features and find places on the globe • develop some awareness of weather and climate in other parts of the world • develop some awareness of the types of environment which exist in other parts of the world
		5th/6th Class	• become familiar with the natural and human features of some places in other parts of the world • acquire an understanding of the relative location and size of major natural and human features • begin to develop an understanding of the names and relative location of some natural and human features of the world • develop some awareness of directions in wider environments • develop familiarity with, and engage in practical use of, maps • develop an understanding of and use common map features and conventions • recognise key lines of latitude and longitude on the globe • study some aspects of the environments and lives of people in one location in another part of the world • become familiar with the names and approximate location of a small number of major world physical features • become aware of the characteristics of some major climatic regions in different parts of the world

CURRICULUM LINKS

COUNTRY	SUBJECT	LEVEL	OBJECTIVES
Scotland	Social Studies	First	• explore climate zones around the world, and describe how climate affects living things • explore a natural environment different from their own, and discover how the physical features influence the variety of living things
		Second	• study a contrasting area outwith Britain and investigate the main features of weather and climate, discussing the impact on living things • interpret information from different maps, and locate key features within the UK, Europe or wider world
Wales	Geography	KS 2	• identify and locate places and environments using globes, atlases and maps • identify and describe natural and human features • identify similarities and differences to describe, compare and contrast places and environments • study living in other countries – contrasting localities outside the United Kingdom

NOTES

What's in this book

▶ **5 sections** of reproducible information and activity pages centred on five main topics: Asia in the world, Political divisions, Physical features, Valuable resources and Culture.

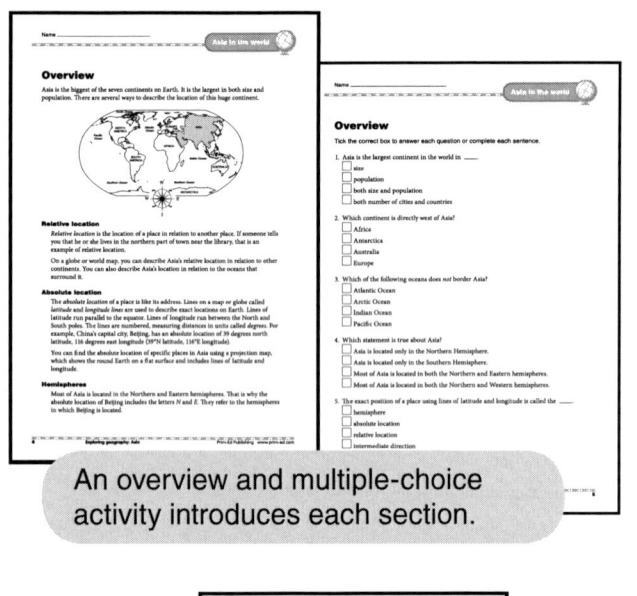

An overview and multiple-choice activity introduces each section.

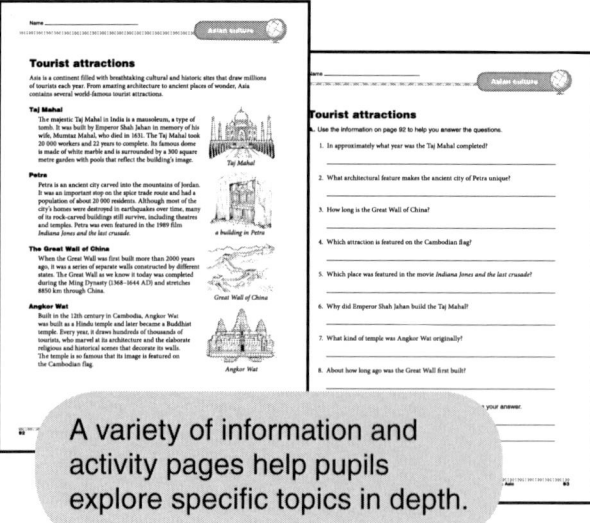

A variety of information and activity pages help pupils explore specific topics in depth.

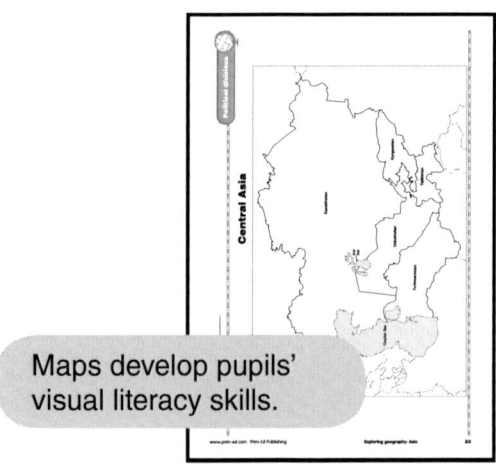

Maps develop pupils' visual literacy skills.

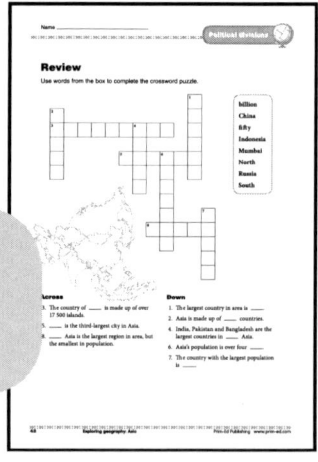

A crossword puzzle at the end of each section provides a fun review activity.

▶ **1 section** of assessment activities

▶ **1 section** of open-ended note-takers

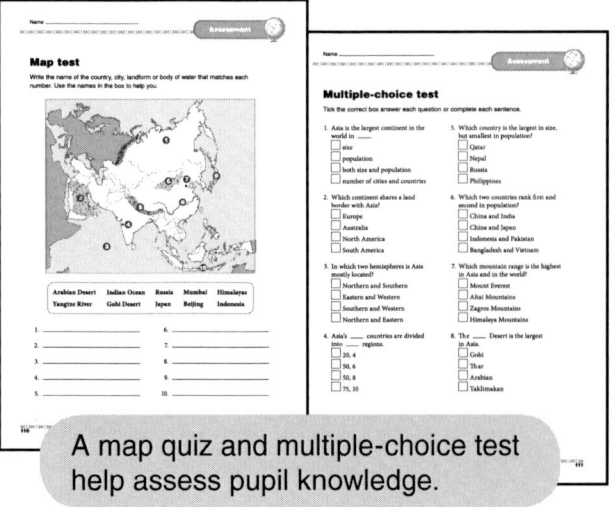

A map quiz and multiple-choice test help assess pupil knowledge.

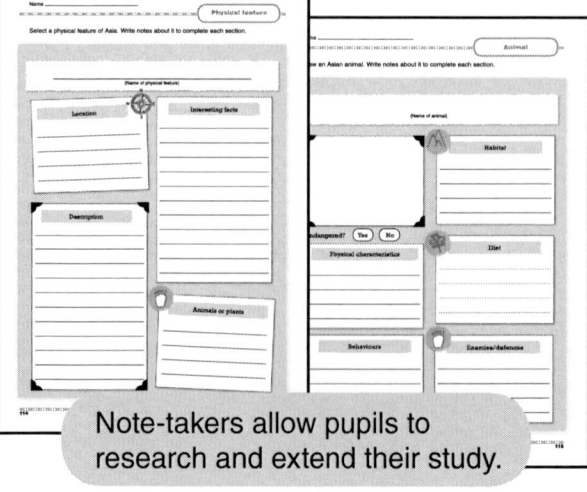

Note-takers allow pupils to research and extend their study.

Asia in the world

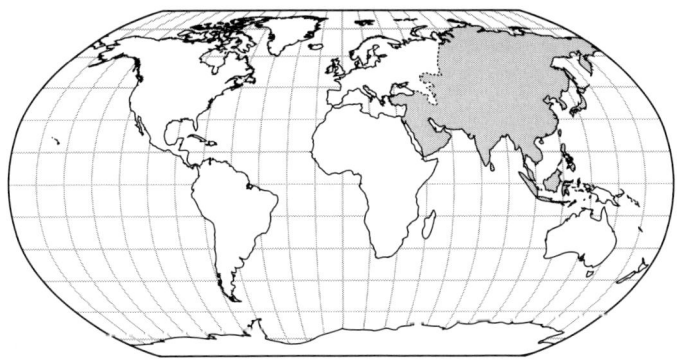

This section introduces pupils to the location of Asia in the world. Pupils learn about the difference between relative and absolute location, as well as the hemispheres in which Asia lies. Pupils also practise using lines of latitude and longitude to find places on a map.

CONTENTS

Overview 6–7	Asia's absolute location 12–13
Asia's relative location 8–9	Using a projection map 14–15
Asia's hemispheres 10–11	Review 16

Name _____

Asia in the world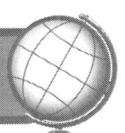

Overview

Asia is the biggest of the seven continents on Earth. It is the largest in both size and population. There are several ways to describe the location of this huge continent.

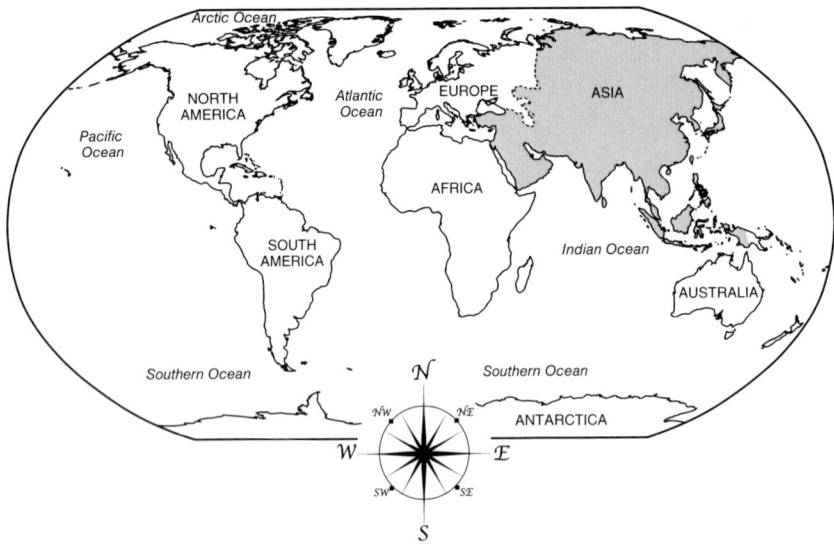

Relative location

Relative location is the location of a place in relation to another place. If someone tells you that he or she lives in the northern part of town near the library, that is an example of relative location.

On a globe or world map, you can describe Asia's relative location in relation to other continents. You can also describe Asia's location in relation to the oceans that surround it.

Absolute location

The *absolute location* of a place is like its address. Lines on a map or globe called *latitude* and *longitude lines* are used to describe exact locations on Earth. Lines of latitude run parallel to the equator. Lines of longitude run between the North and South poles. The lines are numbered, measuring distances in units called *degrees*. For example, China's capital city, Beijing, has an absolute location of 39 degrees north latitude, 116 degrees east longitude (39°N latitude, 116°E longitude).

You can find the absolute location of specific places in Asia using a projection map, which shows the round Earth on a flat surface and includes lines of latitude and longitude.

Hemispheres

Most of Asia is located in the Northern and Eastern hemispheres. That is why the absolute location of Beijing includes the letters *N* and *E*. They refer to the hemispheres in which Beijing is located.

Name _____

Asia in the world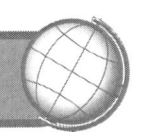

Overview

Tick the correct box to answer each question or complete each sentence.

1. Asia is the largest continent in the world in ____.
   ☐ size
   ☐ population
   ☐ both size and population
   ☐ both number of cities and countries

2. Which continent is directly west of Asia?
   ☐ Africa
   ☐ Antarctica
   ☐ Australia
   ☐ Europe

3. Which of the following oceans does *not* border Asia?
   ☐ Atlantic Ocean
   ☐ Arctic Ocean
   ☐ Indian Ocean
   ☐ Pacific Ocean

4. Which statement is true about Asia?
   ☐ Asia is located only in the Northern Hemisphere.
   ☐ Asia is located only in the Southern Hemisphere.
   ☐ Most of Asia is located in both the Northern and Eastern hemispheres.
   ☐ Most of Asia is located in both the Northern and Western hemispheres.

5. The exact position of a place using lines of latitude and longitude is called the ____.
   ☐ hemisphere
   ☐ absolute location
   ☐ relative location
   ☐ intermediate direction

Name _____

Asia in the world

Asia's relative location

Relative location is the position of a place in relation to another place. How would you describe where Asia is located in the world using relative location?

Look at the world map on page 9. One way to describe Asia's relative location is to name the other continents that border it. For example, Asia is east of Europe and north of Australia. Central Asia is north-east of Africa.

Another way to describe the relative location of Asia is to name the oceans that surround the continent. The frigid Arctic Ocean borders Asia to the north. To the south is the warm Indian Ocean. The vast Pacific Ocean borders Asia to the east.

A. Use the map on page 9 to complete the paragraph about the relative location of Asia.

Asia is the largest continent in the entire world. It is located east of the continent of _____ and north of the island continent of _____. Africa is to the _____ of Central Asia. To the north is the cold _____ Ocean. The Indian Ocean is _____ of Asia. The _____ Ocean borders the continent to the east. Asia is a continent that stretches both long and wide.

B. Follow the directions to colour the map on page 9.

1. Colour the continent west of Asia orange.
2. Use blue to circle the name of the ocean that is east of Asia.
3. Draw a kangaroo next to the island continent south of Asia.

Name _____

Asia in the world

Asia's relative location

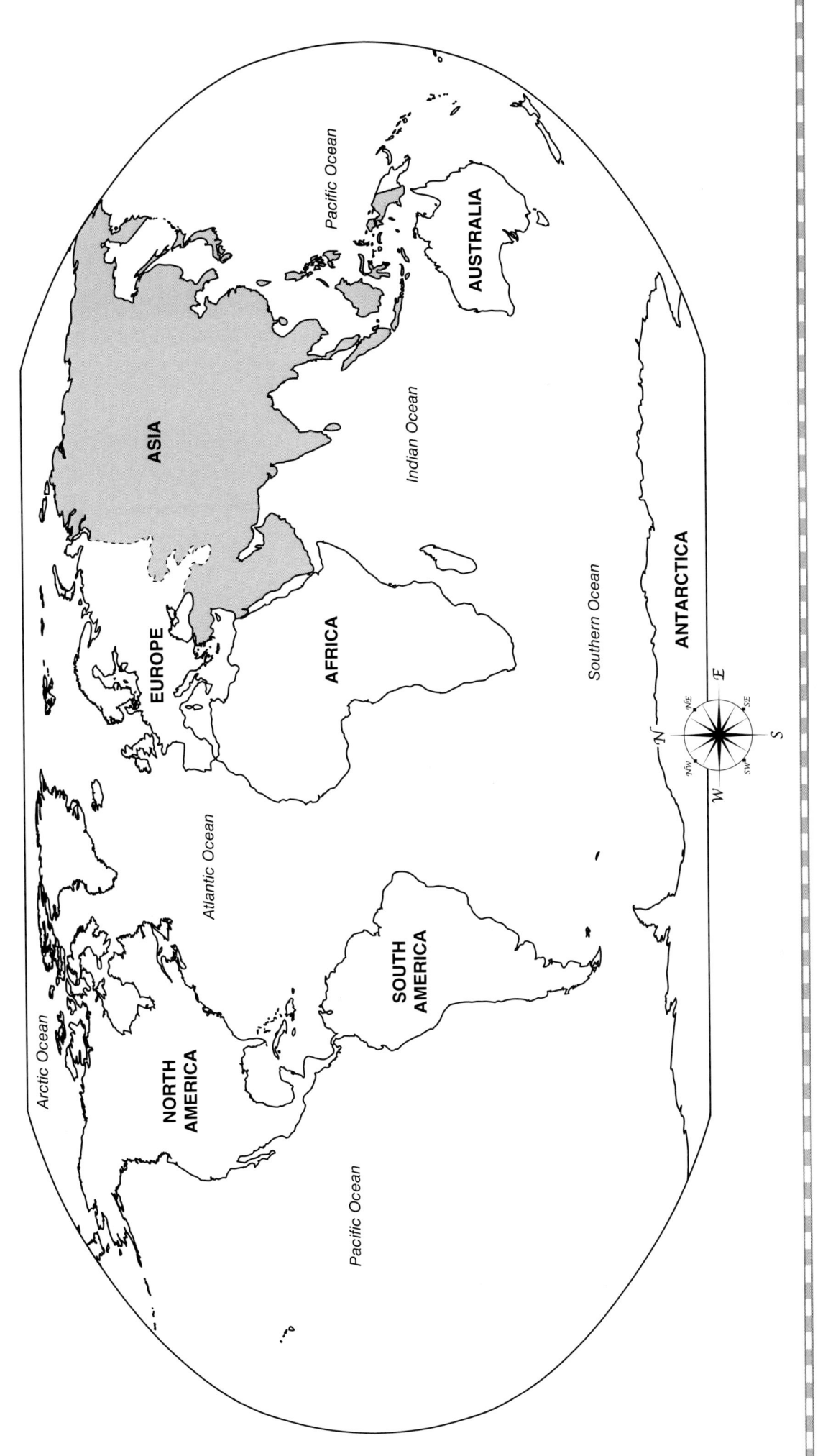

Arctic Ocean
NORTH AMERICA
Atlantic Ocean
EUROPE
ASIA
Pacific Ocean
AFRICA
Indian Ocean
AUSTRALIA
SOUTH AMERICA
Southern Ocean
ANTARCTICA
Pacific Ocean

www.prim-ed.com   Prim-Ed Publishing
Exploring geography: Asia
9

Asia's hemispheres

On a globe, the Earth is divided into four hemispheres by a horizontal line called the *equator* and by vertical lines that run from the North Pole to the South Pole. The hemispheres are the Northern, Southern, Western and Eastern. Most of Asia is part of the Northern hemisphere because the majority of the continent is north of the equator. A small part of Asia is located south of the equator, so that part is in the Southern hemisphere. Asia is also located in the Eastern hemisphere.

Northern and Southern hemispheres

A globe shows an imaginary horizontal line that runs around the centre of the Earth. This line is called the equator. The equator divides the Earth into the Northern and Southern hemispheres.

Since most of Asia is north of the equator, the continent is in the Northern Hemisphere.

Western and Eastern hemispheres

A globe also shows imaginary vertical lines that run from the North Pole to the South Pole. One of these vertical lines is called the *prime meridian*. This line, along with its twin line on the opposite side of the globe, create the Western and Eastern hemispheres.

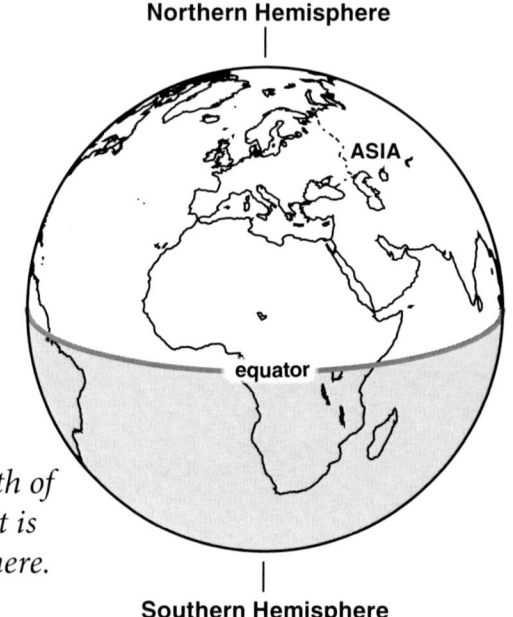

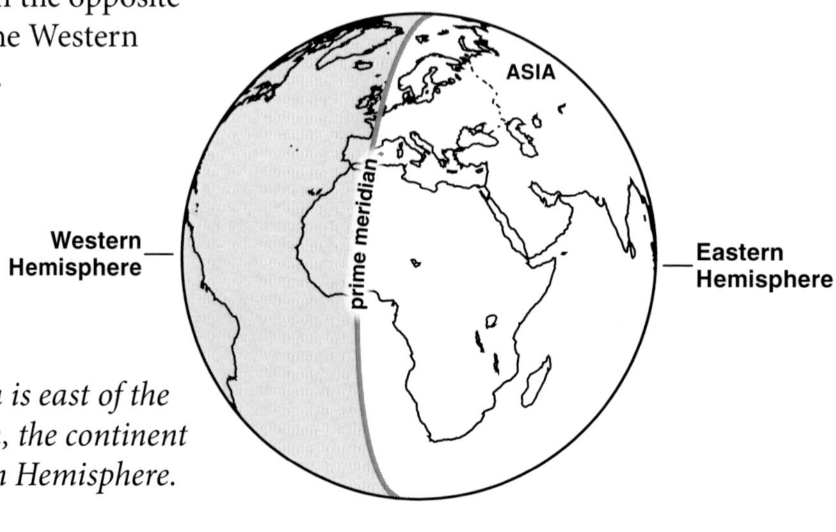

Since all of Asia is east of the prime meridian, the continent is in the Eastern Hemisphere.

Asia's hemispheres

A. Write the letter of the definition that matches each term. Use the information and pictures of the globes on page 10 to help you.

____ 1. Asia

____ 2. continent

____ 3. globe

____ 4. equator

____ 5. Eastern Hemisphere

____ 6. hemisphere

____ 7. North Pole

____ 8. Northern Hemisphere

____ 9. prime meridian

a. an imaginary line that runs from the North Pole to the South Pole

b. half of the Earth

c. the continent that is mostly in the Northern and Eastern hemispheres

d. the hemisphere that is east of the prime meridian

e. an imaginary line that divides the Earth into the Northern and Southern hemispheres

f. any of the seven large landmasses of Earth

g. the northernmost point on Earth

h. a round model of the Earth

i. the hemisphere that is north of the equator

B. Label the parts of the globe. Use the letters next to the terms in the box.

A. Southern Hemisphere

B. Asia

C. Northern Hemisphere

D. Eastern Hemisphere

E. equator

F. prime meridian

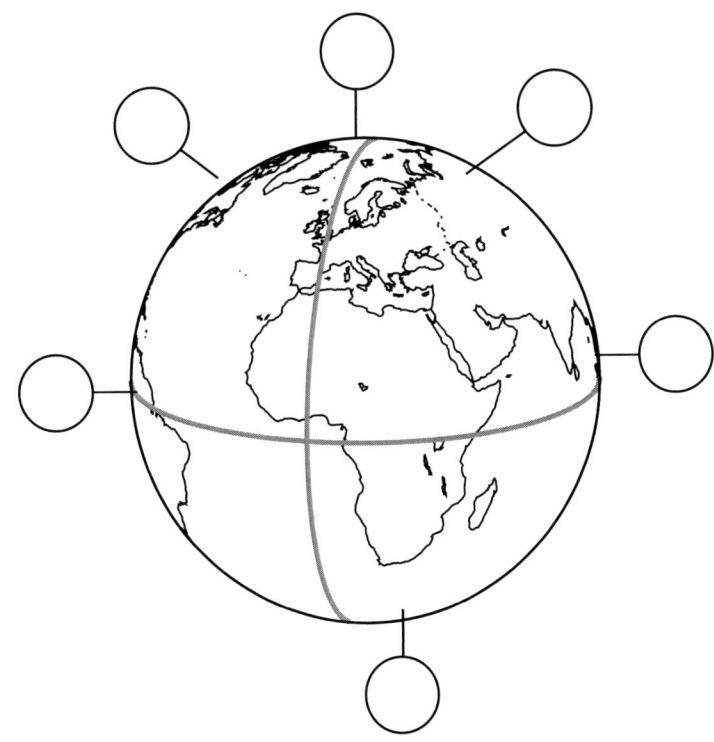

Name _____

Asia in the world

Asia's absolute location

Many globes contain lines that make it easier to find specific places on Earth. Lines of latitude measure the distance north and south of the equator. Lines of longitude measure the distance east and west of the prime meridian. You can use lines of latitude and longitude to find the absolute location of Asia on a globe.

Latitude

The equator is found at the absolute location of 0° (zero degrees) latitude. Other lines of latitude run parallel to the equator and are labelled with an *N* or *S*, depending on whether they are north or south of the equator. Latitude lines are also called *parallels*.

On the picture of the globe, notice the lines of latitude. Look for the continent of Asia. Since most of the continent is north of the equator, most of the latitude lines used to find the absolute location of places within Asia are labelled in *degrees north*, or °N.

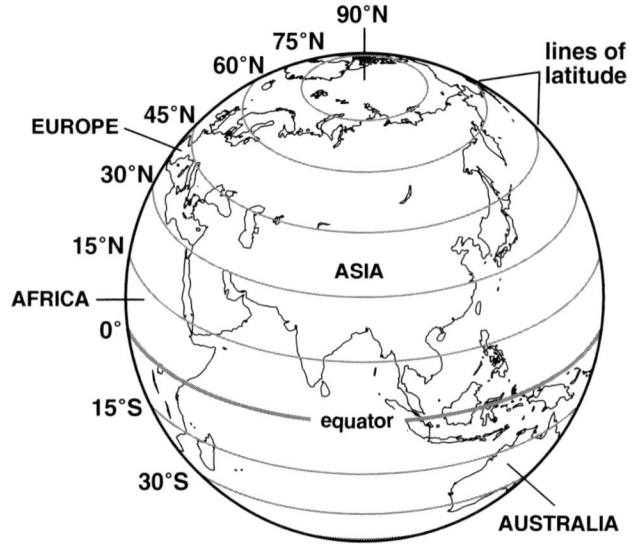

Lines of latitude (parallels)

Longitude

The prime meridian runs from the North Pole to the South Pole at 0° (zero degrees) longitude. Other lines of longitude run north and south, too and are labelled with an *E* or *W*, depending on whether they are east or west of the prime meridian. Longitude lines are also called *meridians*.

On the picture of the globe, notice the lines of longitude. Look for the entire continent of Asia. Since the entire continent is east of the prime meridian, all of the longitude lines used to find the absolute location of places within Asia are labelled in *degrees east*, or °E.

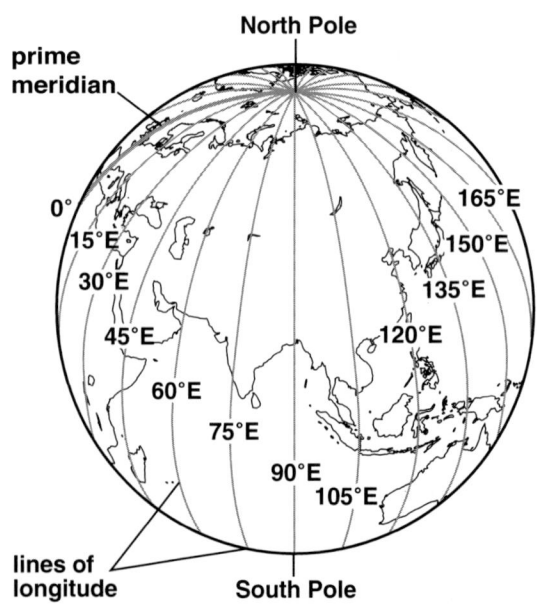

Lines of longitude (meridians)

12 Exploring geography: Asia   Prim-Ed Publishing www.prim-ed.com

Name _____

Asia in the world

Asia's absolute location

To find the absolute location of a place, read the latitude line first, then read the longitude line. For example, the latitude 30°N runs through the southern part of China. The longitude 90°E runs through the western part of China. So the absolute location of South-West China is 30°N latitude, 90°E longitude.

A. Circle the answer to each question. Use the pictures of the globes and information on page 12 to help you.

1. Which line is at 0 degrees latitude?	equator	prime meridian
2. Which line runs north and south?	equator	prime meridian
3. In which direction is most of Asia from the equator?	north	south
4. Which line of longitude runs through Asia?	75°E	75°W
5. Where is the North Pole located?	90°S	90°N
6. Which lines run parallel to the equator?	latitude lines	longitude lines
7. How many degrees are between each line of latitude and longitude on the globes?	10 degrees	15 degrees
8. What is another name for *lines of latitude*?	meridians	parallels
9. Which line of latitude runs through Asia?	30°N	30°S
10. What is another name for *lines of longitude*?	parallels	meridians

B. Using the information on page 12, explain why most places in Asia have absolute locations that are labelled in degrees north and east.

_____

_____

www.prim-ed.com Prim-Ed Publishing   Exploring geography: Asia 13

Name _____

Asia in the world

Using a projection map

How do you draw a picture of a round object, such as the Earth, on a flat piece of paper? In order to show all of Earth's continents and oceans in one view, mapmakers use a system called *projection*. Mapping the round Earth on a flat surface causes some areas to look bigger than they really are. For example, land near the poles gets stretched out when flattened. That's why Greenland and Antarctica look so big on some maps.

A projection map of the world shows all the lines of latitude and longitude on Earth. Study the projection map on page 15. Notice the lines of latitude and longitude. You can use these lines to find the absolute location of a specific place in Asia. For example, the label *Asia* is located at 50°N latitude, 90°E longitude.

A. Read each statement. Circle **yes** if it is true or **no** if it is false. Use the map on page 15 to help you.

1. Asia is located on the prime meridian.   **Yes**   **No**

2. Most of Asia is located between the longitudes of 45°E and 170°E.   **Yes**   **No**

3. All of Asia is located between the latitudes of 60°N and 75°N.   **Yes**   **No**

4. Asia is the only continent east of the prime meridian.   **Yes**   **No**

5. Asia shares some of the same north latitude lines with Europe.   **Yes**   **No**

6. The longitude line 90°E runs through Asia and Australia.   **Yes**   **No**

7. The latitude line 30°N runs through Africa and Asia.   **Yes**   **No**

8. Part of Asia is located on the latitude line 30°S.   **Yes**   **No**

9. There are no continents on 60°N latitude.   **Yes**   **No**

B. How many continents can you find on the map that are on the longitude line 120°E? Write their names.

_____

_____

Using a projection map

Asia in the world

Name _____

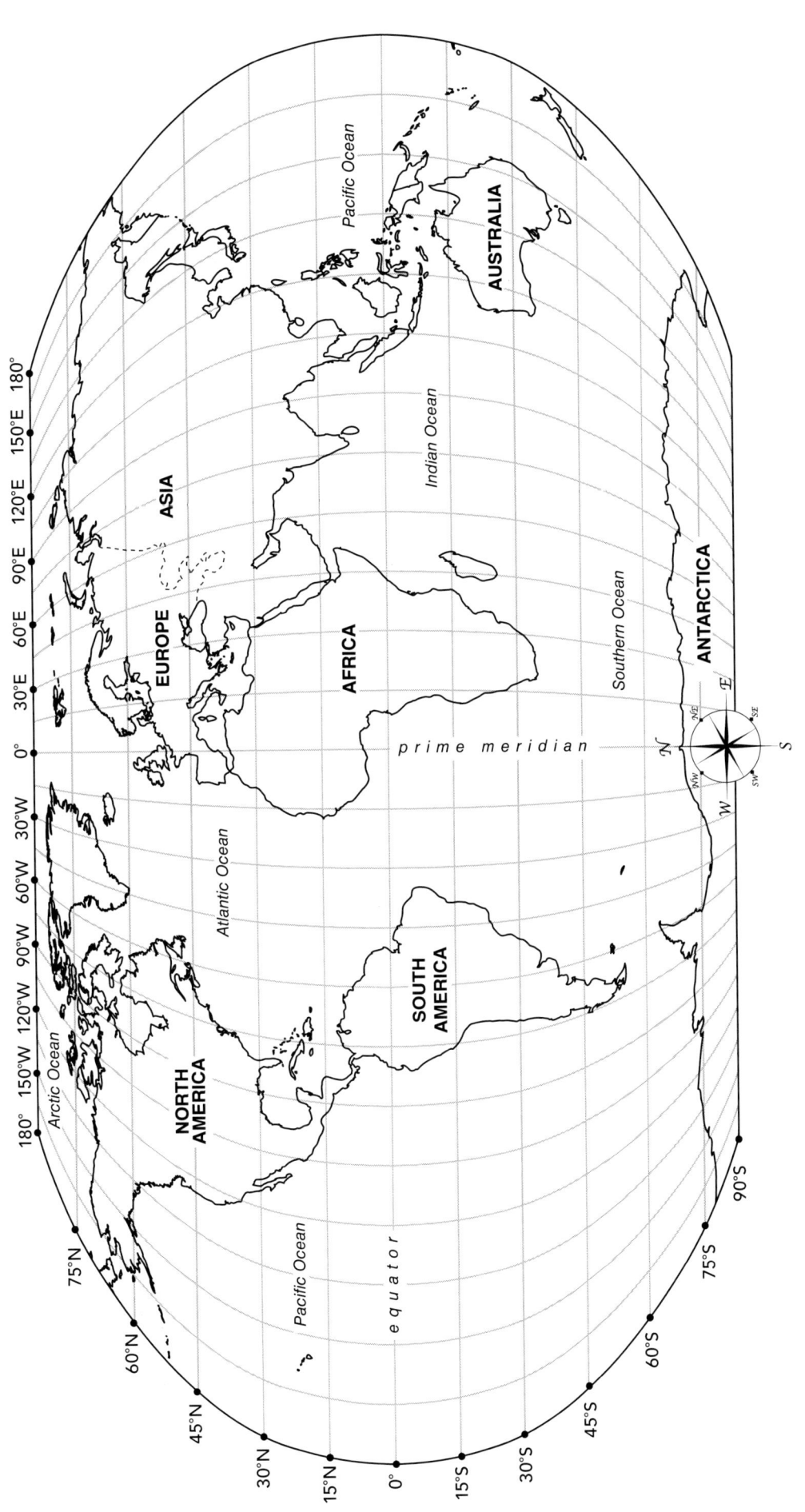

Review

Use words from the box to complete the crossword puzzle.

Word box:
- Africa
- Asia
- equator
- Europe
- hemispheres
- Pacific
- projection
- relative

Across

1. The Arctic, Indian and ____ oceans border Asia.
5. If you go south-west of the centre of Asia, you will find the continent of ____.
6. Most of Asia is part of the Northern and Eastern ____.
7. ____ location is a description of a place in relation to another place.
8. The ____ is the imaginary line that divides the Earth into the Northern and Southern hemispheres.

Down

2. ____ is the largest continent in the world.
3. The continent of ____ is west of Asia.
4. A ____ map shows the round Earth on a flat surface.

Political divisions of Asia

This section introduces pupils to the six regions and 50 countries of Asia. Pupils learn how the regions differ in size and population, studying data about the largest countries and cities within each region. Pupils also learn that Asia is now, and will probably continue to be, the most populated continent in the world.

CONTENTS

Overview 18–19	South Asia 30–31
Population of Asia 20–21	Central Asia 32–33
Countries of Asia 22–23	North Asia 34–35
Largest countries by area . . . 24–25	East Asia 36–37
Largest countries by population 26–27	South-East Asia 38–39
	Largest cities of Asia 40–41
South-West Asia 28–29	Review 42

Name _____

Political divisions

Overview

Asia is the largest continent on Earth in both size and population.

- Asia makes up about 30% of the world's landmass.
- Asia has about 60% of the world's people—4 billion.

The six regions

The 50 countries of Asia are divided into six regions.

Region	Number of countries	Fast facts
South-West Asia	20	also called the Middle East
South Asia	7	includes the second most populated country (India)
Central Asia	5	countries that were once part of Russia
North Asia	1	the largest region in terms of land area (Russia)
East Asia	6	includes the country with the largest population (China)
South-East Asia	11	some countries in this region are islands

Where people live

Most people in Asia live in river valleys or near seacoasts. But Asia also has some of the largest, most densely populated cities in the world. Tokyo, Japan, is the world's most populated metropolitan area. Tokyo has more than 36 million people living in the city and surrounding areas. Some other huge cities are Mumbai, India; Delhi, India; Seoul, South Korea; Shanghai, China; and Jakarta, Indonesia.

Population experts predict that by 2050, the world will have about 9 billion people. Of that 9 billion, over 5 billion will be living in Asia. Asia will retain its ranking as the largest continent in both size and population for a long time.

Name _____

Political divisions

Overview

Tick the correct box to answer each question or complete each sentence.

1. Asia has ____ countries that are divided into ____ regions.
   - ☐ 11, 4
   - ☐ 20, 5
   - ☐ 35, 6
   - ☐ 50, 6

2. Which region of Asia has the most countries?
   - ☐ North Asia
   - ☐ South Asia
   - ☐ South-West Asia
   - ☐ South-East Asia

3. The north region contains the country of ____.
   - ☐ China
   - ☐ Russia
   - ☐ Indonesia
   - ☐ South Korea

4. The most populated metropolitan area in the world is ____.
   - ☐ Mumbai, India
   - ☐ Tokyo, Japan
   - ☐ Shanghai, China
   - ☐ Jakarta, Indonesia

5. Which statement is true about Asia's population?
   - ☐ Asia has 4 billion people and it is expected to grow to 5 billion by 2050.
   - ☐ Asia has 4 billion people and it will remain at that number in 2050.
   - ☐ Asia has 9 billion people and it is expected to double in population by 2050.
   - ☐ Asia is the largest continent in both size and population, but its ranking will change in 2050.

Population of Asia

A *population census* is a survey by a national government to gather information about the number of people who live in a country. Population censuses have been conducted since ancient times. The earliest known population counts were made by the Chinese and Egyptians. Most countries in modern history conduct an official census every 10 years. In addition, experts look at the data from the past to predict what the population will be in the future.

Throughout modern history, Asia has had the largest population of all seven continents. In 1950, Asia's population was about 1.4 billion. By 2010, the population of Asia stood at over 4 billion. By comparison, Africa has the next-largest population of all the continents with about 1 billion people. According to census data, Asia's population will continue to grow steadily, reaching more than 5 billion by 2050.

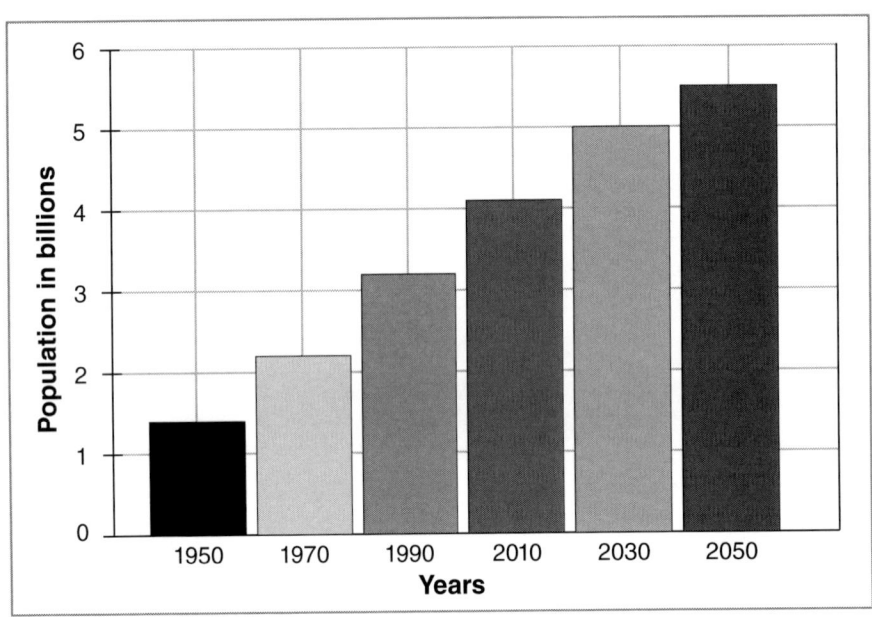

US Bureau of the Census, International Data Base

A. Use the information above to write a caption for the bar graph. Include at least two interesting facts.

_____

_____

_____

Name _____

Political divisions

Population of Asia

B. Read each statement. Circle **yes** if it is true or **no** if it is false. Use the information on page 20 to help you.

1. The graph shows population growth over a 100-year span.   Yes   No

2. In 1950, Asia had a population of exactly 1 billion.   Yes   No

3. From 1950 to 2010, there was a steady increase in population.   Yes   No

4. In 1970, Asia's population jumped to more than 2 billion.   Yes   No

5. In 1990, Asia's population was 4 billion.   Yes   No

6. From 1970 to 1990, Asia's population increased by about 1 billion.   Yes   No

7. Projections show that Asia will have a population of 5 billion in 2030.   Yes   No

8. From 2030 to 2050, Asia's population will decrease by 500 million.   Yes   No

9. The bar graph shows population growth figures in 20-year segments.   Yes   No

10. The bar graph shows that after 2050, Asia's population will start to decrease.   Yes   No

C. Use the information in the bar graph to answer the questions. Circle the answer.

1. During which 20-year period did the population increase the most?

   1950–1970   **1970–1990**   **1990–2010**

2. What would you predict the population of Asia to be in 2070?

   8 billion   **less than 5 billion**   **more than 6 billion**

Name _____

Political divisions

Countries of Asia

Asia is made up of 50 countries. Some are large in population. China and India are the most populated countries of Asia. Some countries are large in size, such as Russia and China, and some are small island nations, such as Brunei and Timor-Leste.

A. Read the names of the Asian countries. Notice there are asterisks (*) after four countries. Read the footnotes below the list to learn how these countries are unique.

Afghanistan	Indonesia	Mongolia	Sri Lanka
Armenia	Iran	Myanmar (Burma)	Syria
Azerbaijan	Iraq	Nepal	Taiwan***
Bahrain	Israel	North Korea	Tajikistan
Bangladesh	Japan	Oman	Thailand
Bhutan	Jordan	Pakistan	Timor-Leste (East Timor)
Brunei	Kazakhstan	Philippines	Turkey**
Cambodia	Kuwait	Qatar	Turkmenistan
China	Kyrgyzstan	Russia**	United Arab Emirates (UAE)
Cyprus	Laos	Saudi Arabia	Uzbekistan
Egypt*	Lebanon	Singapore	Vietnam
Georgia	Malaysia	South Korea	Yemen
India	Maldives		

  * The country of Egypt is also included on the list of countries in Africa. Egypt lies mostly in Africa. However, the north-east corner of Egypt is called the Sinai Peninsula. The Sinai Peninsula is considered part of South-West Asia.

  ** The countries of Russia and Turkey lie mostly in Asia, so they have been included in the total number of Asian countries. However, parts of these countries also lie in Europe.

  *** It is disputed whether Taiwan is an independent country. Taiwan considers itself an independent country. China claims that Taiwan is part of China.

B. Look at the political map of Asia on page 23. Find the following five countries and colour each one a different colour.

> **Mongolia**   **South Korea**   **Sri Lanka**   **Turkey**   **Yemen**

Political divisions

Countries of Asia

Name _____

Name _____

Political divisions

Largest countries by area

Asia has some of the world's largest countries in terms of square kilometres. In fact, of the 10 largest countries in the world, four are located in Asia.

The five largest countries of Asia (listed in alphabetical order) are:

China:	9 596 961 square km
India:	3 287 263 square km
Kazakhstan:	2 724 900 square km
Russia (Asian part):	12 788 842 square km
Saudi Arabia:	2 149 690 square km

A. Fill in the chart to rank the five largest countries from **1** to **5**, with **1** being the largest.

Rank in size	Country	Square kilometres
1		
2		
3		
4		
5		

B. On the map on page 25, you will see five numbered countries. The numbers indicate the rank of each country according to size. Colour each country a different colour. Then complete the map key by writing the country names in order from largest to smallest. Write the colour you used on the map for each country.

Name _____

Political divisions

Largest countries by area

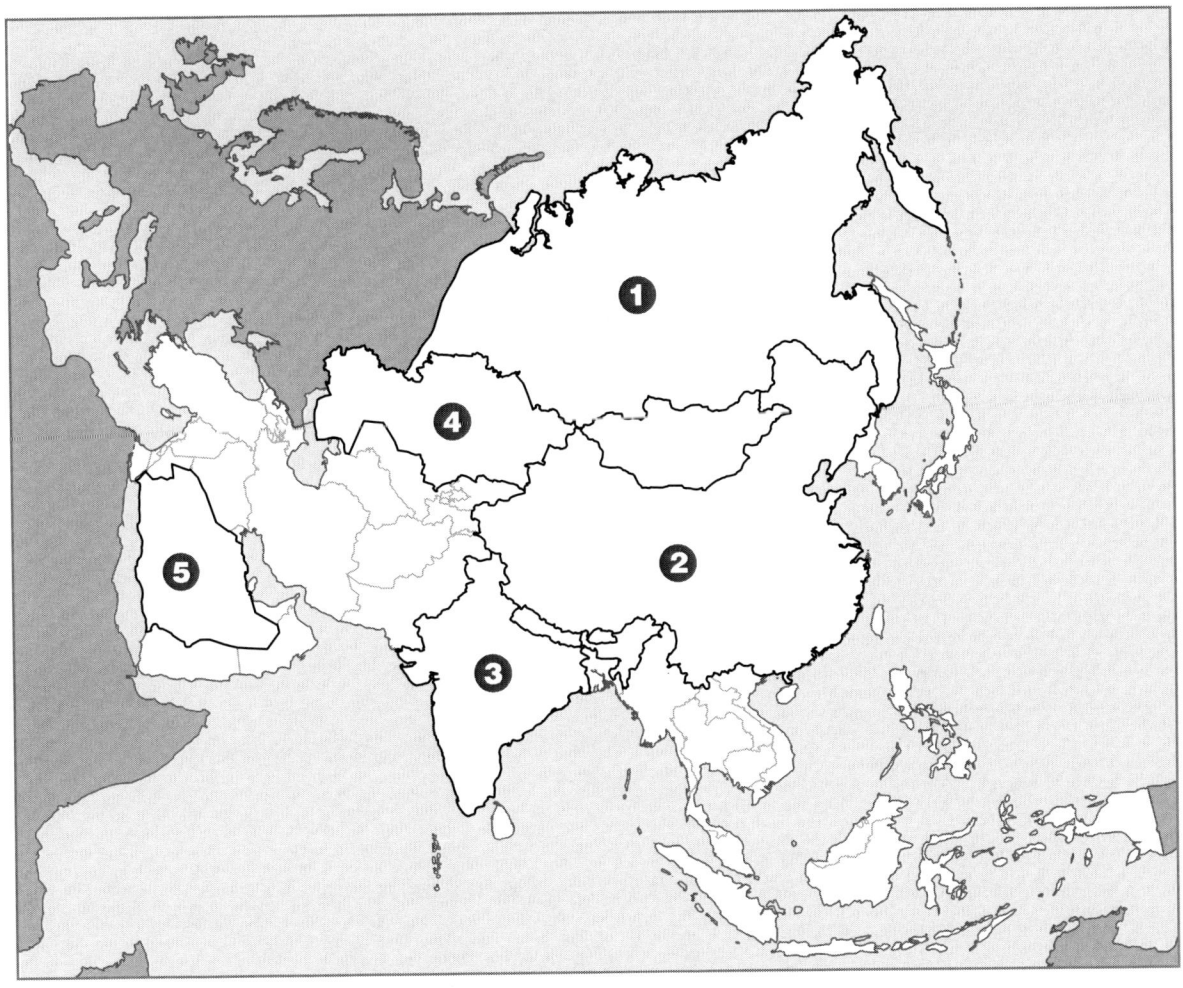

MAP KEY

The five largest countries   Colour

1. _____   _____

2. _____   _____

3. _____   _____

4. _____   _____

5. _____   _____

Largest countries by population

Asia's population is not only the largest of all the continents, but it also has some of the most populated countries. In fact, both China and India have bigger populations than the entire continent of Africa!

Two ways to read large population numbers are by standard form and by word form. For example, 1 355 350 000 is written in standard form. In word form, the number is written out like this: 1 billion, 355 million, 350 thousand.

Most populated countries of Asia

Rank	Country	Population
1	China	1 349 585 000 (1 billion, 349 million, 585 thousand)
2	India	1 220 800 000 (1 billion, 220 million, 800 thousand)
3	Indonesia	251 160 000 (251 million, 160 thousand)
4	Pakistan	193 238 000 (193 million, 238 thousand)
5	Bangladesh	163 654 000 (163 million, 654 thousand)
6	Japan	127 253 000 (127 million, 253 thousand)
7	Philippines	105 720 000 (105 million, 720 thousand)
8	Vietnam	92 477 000 (92 million, 477 thousand)
9	Iran	79 853 000 (79 million, 853 thousand)
10	Myanmar	55 167 000 (55 million, 167 thousand)

Populations are 2013 estimates based on figures from official US Government sources.

Name _____

Political divisions

Largest countries by population

A. Look at the chart on page 26. Notice that the population figures are written in both standard form and word form. Use the information in the chart to answer the questions.

1. How many countries have a population of over 1 billion? _____

2. Which country has a population of 79 million, 853 thousand? _____

3. How many countries have a population of under 100 000 000? _____

4. What is the population of Japan? Write it in word form.

   _____

5. Which countries rank 1st and 10th in population?

   1st: _____ 10th: _____

6. Which country has a population of 193 238 000?

   _____

7. What is the difference in population between China and India? Write the answer in standard form.

   _____

B. When reading the chart on page 26, remember that population figures are always changing. The population figures on that page are for 2013. Look at the population clocks for the UK and Ireland on the following websites:
UK: http://countrymeters.info/en/United_Kingdom_(UK)/
Ireland: http://countrymeters.info/en/Ireland/
On the day this was written, the UK's population was 63 150 956, and Ireland's 4 656 091.

What is the UK's population right now? _____

What is Ireland's population right now? _____

South-West Asia

South-West Asia is a region that is made up of 20 countries. Sometimes this region is called the Middle East. Some countries in this region are large in size, such as Saudi Arabia, Iran and Turkey. Some are very small, such as Cyprus, Lebanon and Qatar.

About 330 million people live in South-West Asia. The most populated countries completely within Asia's boundaries are Afghanistan, Iran, Iraq and Saudi Arabia.

Some well-known cities in this region include Baghdad, Iraq; Istanbul, Turkey; Riyadh, Saudi Arabia; and Tel Aviv, Israel.

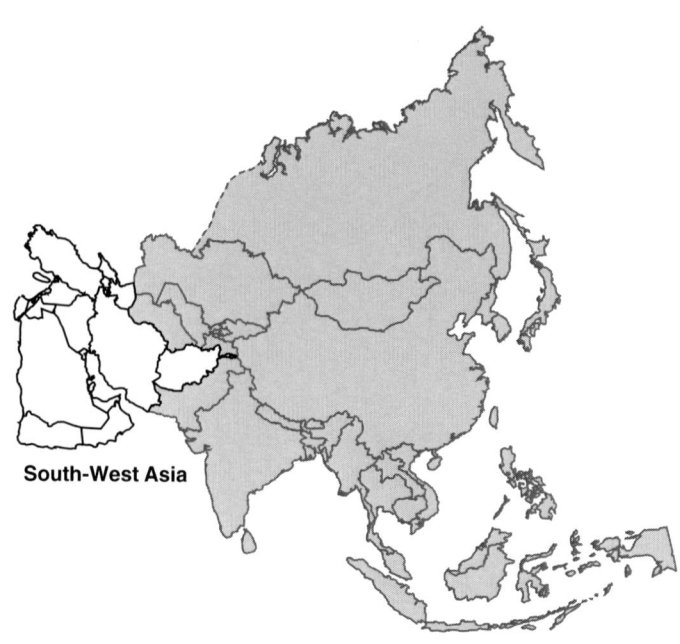

South-West Asia

A. Find and circle the names of the South-West Asian countries in the word search. Words may appear across, down or diagonally.

```
U D J U H C J Q N H E U L U A
T E G J I A A J Y L Y O Q B F
H F N Y S R A S V K J I B C G
L W M A R V H R I F L K R U H
D K V Z A R S Y R I A O D A A
T L A U E S A Q A W I F U F N
L T V L L B I S Q L W L Q U I
J C K J S F F N K U W A I T S
Y O K E Y T L M A G L T K C T
R Q R T U R K E Y H Q F T M A
V J W D T J W R Y W G K C O N
N O K E A R S I Z T K F A N U
K T V I P N N V Z Q L G A X K
D K T S N G A O L H J Q A P Y
J P A R I N M V R D T Q D P O
```

- **Afghanistan**
- **Iran**
- **Iraq**
- **Israel**
- **Jordan**
- **Kuwait**
- **Syria**
- **Turkey**

South-West Asia

B. Look at the map of South-West Asia. Colour all 20 countries. Then write a paragraph about the region below. Use the information on page 28 to help you.

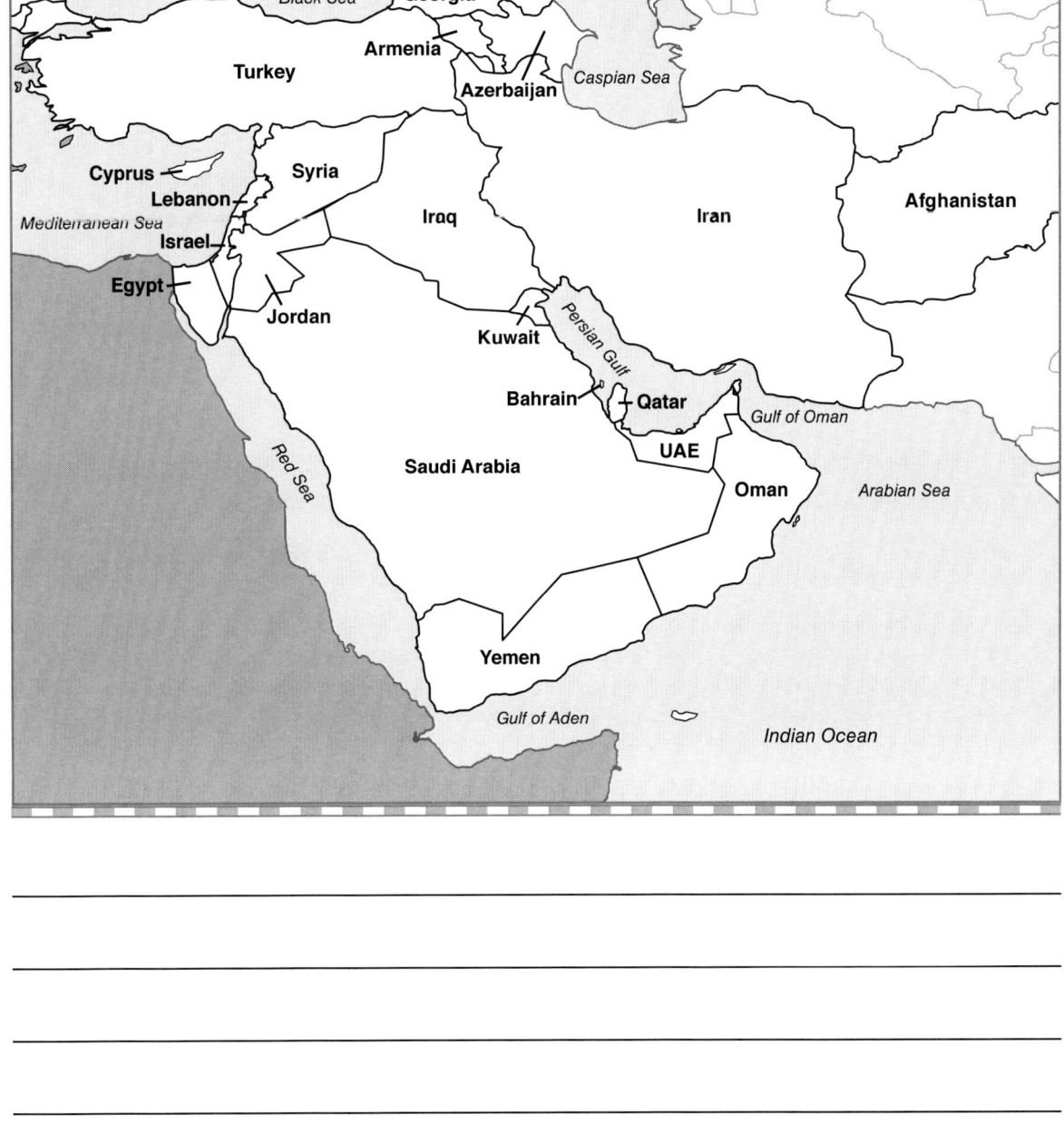

Name _____

Political divisions

South Asia

South Asia is a region that is made up of seven countries. India, Pakistan and Bangladesh are the largest in population. The other four countries—Bhutan, Nepal, the Maldives and Sri Lanka—have large populations, too, but are very small in size.

South Asia is one of the world's most crowded regions. The area has a population of about 1.5 billion. India has the largest population within this region. It is home to more than 1 billion people.

There are several huge, crowded cities in South Asia. Mumbai, India, is one of the largest cities in the world. It has a population of over 19 million.

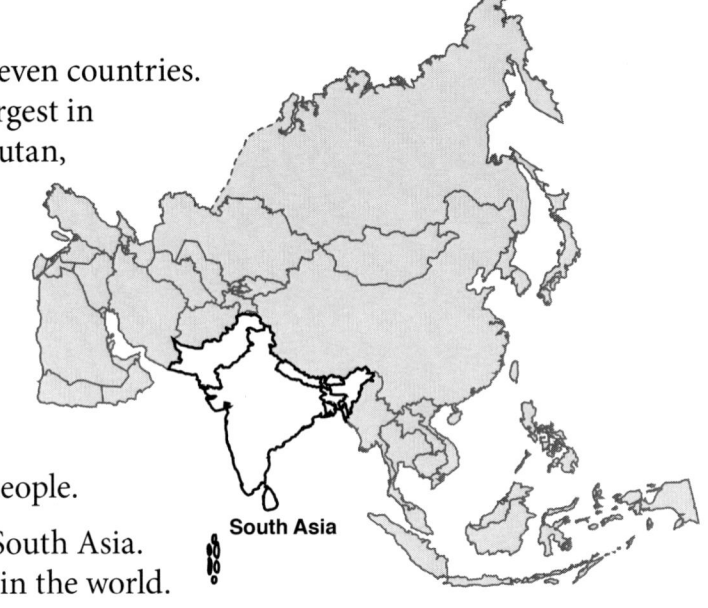
South Asia

A. Complete each sentence by unscrambling the word under the line. Use the information above and the map of South Asia on page 31 to help you.

Some of the answers will need to start with capital letters.

1. South Asia is made up of seven _____.
   setociunr

2. This region is home to more than 1.5 _____ people.
   lboinil

3. The country of _____ has the largest population.
   diina

4. Pakistan is the _____-largest country in size in South Asia.
   ecsnod

5. The largest city in this region is _____.
   baimum

6. The _____ is a country made up of small islands.
   ldviemsa

7. The countries of Pakistan, Nepal, Bhutan and _____ each share a border with India.
   angaldsehb

8. The island nation of _____ is found off the southern tip of India.
   ris kalan

30 Exploring geography: Asia Prim-Ed Publishing www.prim-ed.com

Name _____

Political divisions

South Asia

B. On the map below, use blue to circle the Maldives. Then colour each of the other countries a different colour. Write three facts about South Asia on the lines under the map. Use the information on page 30 to help you.

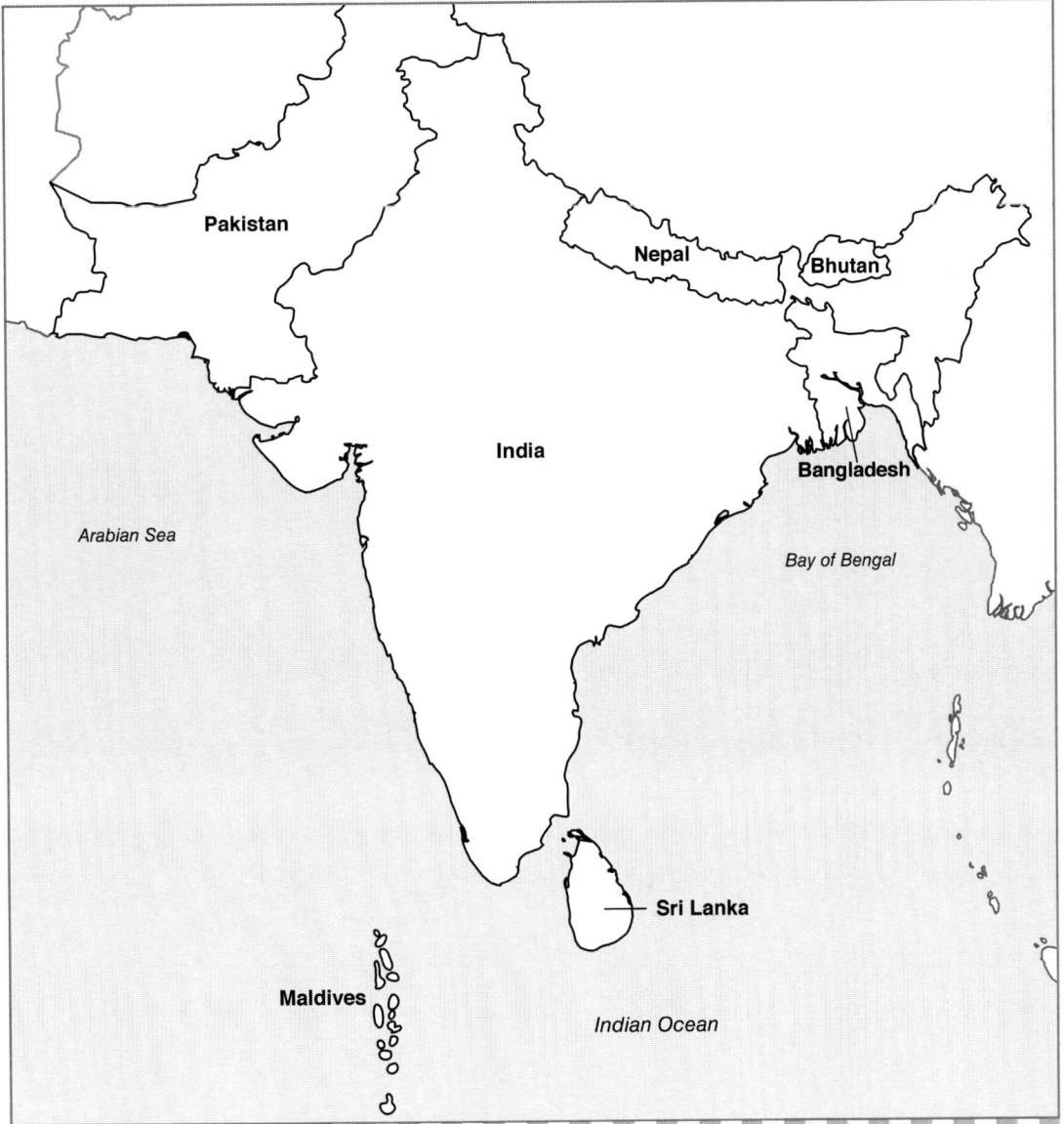

1. _____

2. _____

3. _____

Name _____

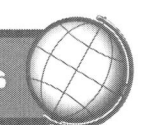

Political divisions

Central Asia

Central Asia is made up of five countries. They are Kazakhstan, Kyrgyzstan, Tajikistan, Turkmenistan and Uzbekistan. (See activity A for pronunciations.) The region is large in size but has a smaller population than other parts of Asia.

About 93 million people, or about 2% of Asia's population, live in Central Asia. Uzbekistan has the largest population, with more than 28 million. The city of Tashkent, Uzbekistan, is the largest in the region. More than 2 million people live in Tashkent.

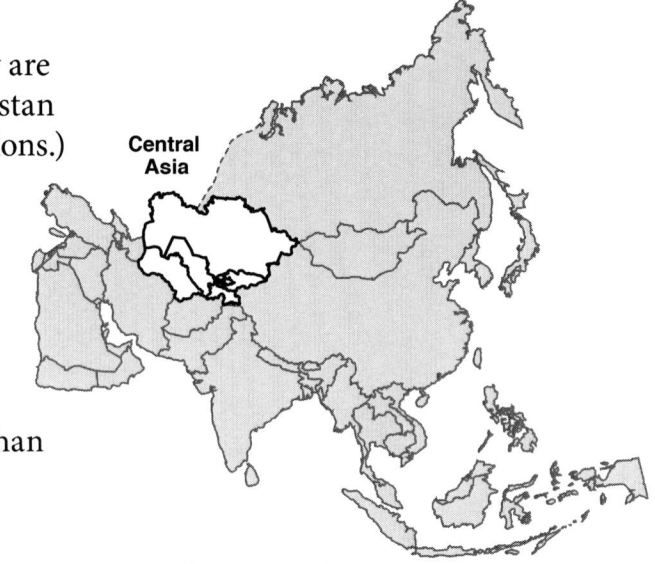

A. The following is a pronunciation key for the countries of Central Asia. Practise saying the country names out loud.

1. Kazakhstan: KUH-zahk-stahn

2. Kyrgyzstan: KER-ghi-stahn

3. Tajikistan: tah-JIK-uh-stahn

4. Turkmenistan: terk-MEN-uh-stahn

5. Uzbekistan: ooz-BEK-uh-stahn

B. Read each question. Fill in the letters to complete the name of the country. Use the information above and the map of Central Asia on page 33 to help you.

1. Which country is the largest in size?   __ __ __ __ __ __ **stan**

2. Which country has the largest population? __ __ __ __ __ __ **stan**

3. The Caspian Sea borders Kazakhstan
   and which other country?   __ __ __ __ __ __ __ __ **stan**

4. Which country does *not* border Kazakhstan? __ __ __ __ __ __ **stan**

5. Tajikistan and which other country are the
   smallest in size?   __ __ __ __ __ **stan**

Political divisions

Central Asia

- Kazakhstan
- Kyrgyzstan
- Tajikistan
- Uzbekistan
- Turkmenistan
- Aral Sea
- Caspian Sea

Name _____

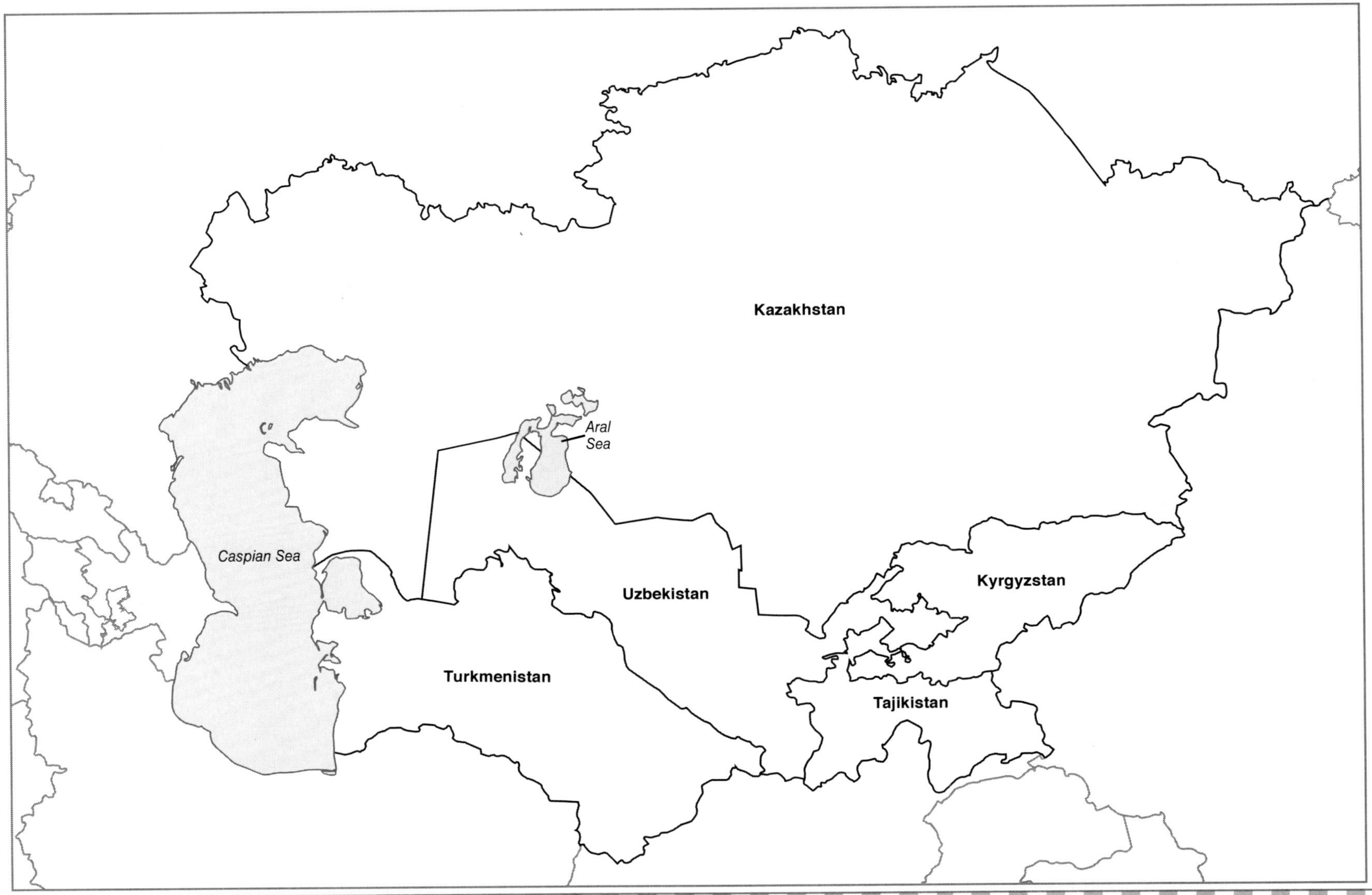

North Asia

North Asia is the largest region in Asia, stretching from the Ural Mountains near Europe to the Pacific Ocean in the east. This vast, cold region covers about 30% of the continent. North Asia is also called Siberia.

The region is unique because it contains only one country—Russia. Russia is so large that three-quarters of it lies in Asia and one-quarter of it lies in Europe.

Although North Asia is the largest region, it has the smallest population. About 37 million people live in Asian Russia. That is only 1% of Asia's total population. Novosibirsk (Noh-vuh-suh-BEARSK) is the largest city in North Asia, with a population of about 1.3 million.

A. Write the missing words on the lines. Use the information above to help you. Then read the paragraphs aloud to a partner.

North Asia is the largest _____ in Asia. Another name for the vast, cold region of North Asia is _____.

It covers about _____% of the continent. Although North Asia is the largest region, it has the smallest _____.

Russia is the only _____ in North Asia. Russia is so large that three-quarters of it lies in Asia and one-quarter lies on the continent of _____. The _____ Mountains form the border between Asian Russia and European Russia. About 37 million people live in Asian Russia. The most populated city in Asian Russian is _____, with a population of about 1.3 million.

North Asia

B. Colour Asian Russia your favourite colour. Then write a paragraph about North Asia on the lines. Use the information on page 34 to help you.

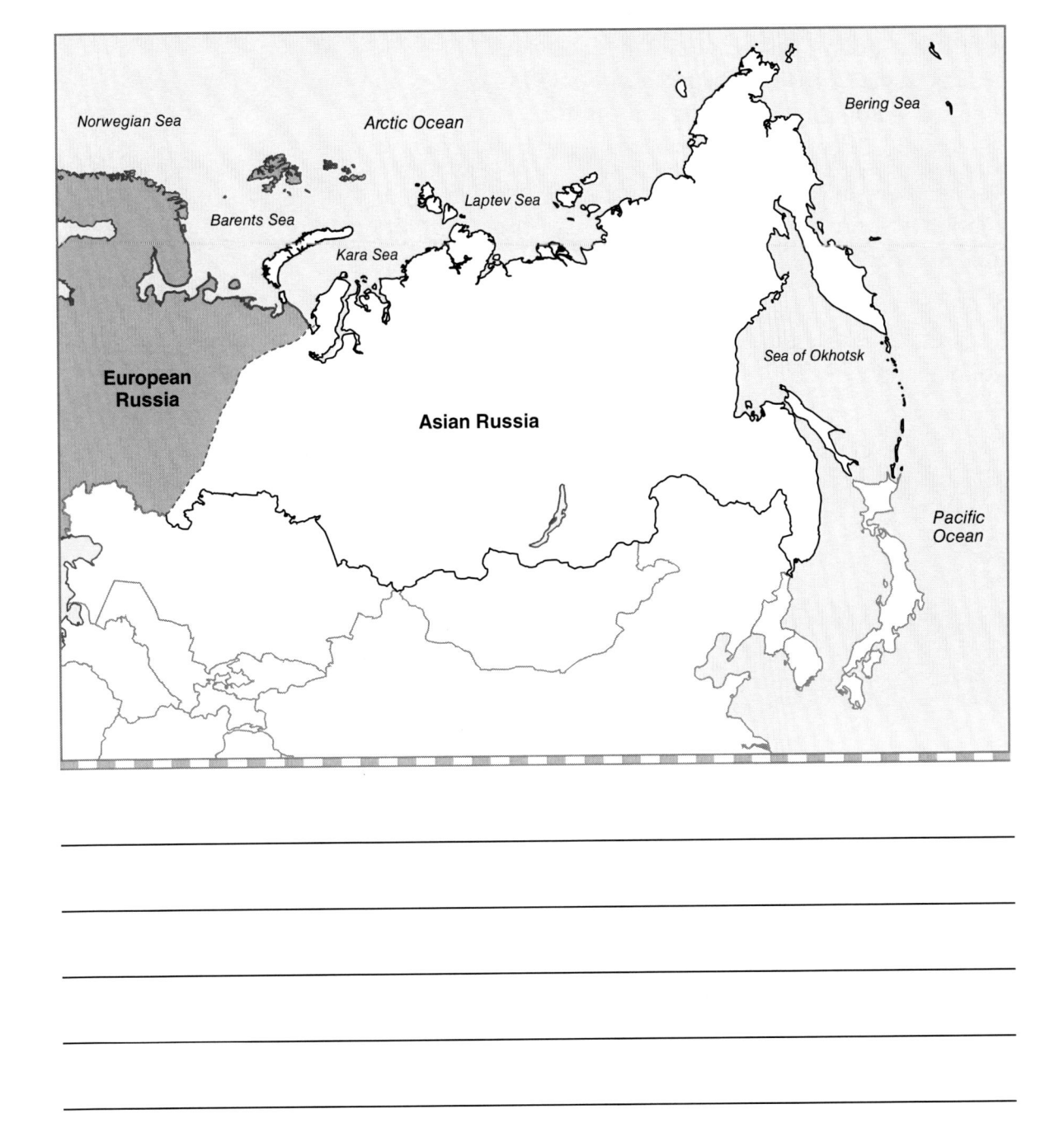

Name _____

Political divisions

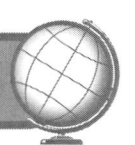

East Asia

East Asia is made up of six countries. They are China, Japan, North Korea, South Korea, Mongolia and Taiwan. China is the largest, covering 90% of East Asia.

More than 1.5 billion people, or 40% of all Asians, live in East Asia. China has the largest population of any country—not only in Asia, but also in the world. It has more than 100 cities that each have over 1 million people.

Tokyo, Japan, is one of the largest capital cities in the region, with a population of more than 36 million. Beijing, China, is another large capital city, with over 12 million residents.

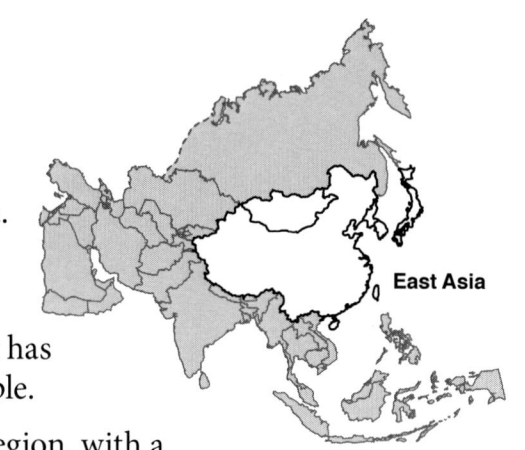

East Asia

A. Look at the chart of East Asian countries and their capital cities, in order from highest population to lowest. Use the information in the chart to answer the questions below.

Country	Capital	Population
Japan	Tokyo	36 507 000
China	Beijing	12 214 000
South Korea	Seoul	9 778 000
North Korea	Pyongyang	2 700 000
Taiwan	Taipei	2 600 000
Mongolia	Ulaanbaatar	949 000

Data taken from CIA Factbook 2013

1. Which capital has the largest population? _____
2. Which capital has the smallest population? _____
3. What is the capital city of South Korea? _____
4. Tokyo is the capital of which country? _____
5. Which capital—Pyongyang or Taipei—has the larger population? _____

B. Using the map of East Asia on page 37, write the name of each country's capital city next to the star. Use the chart on this page to help you. Then colour each country a different colour.

Political divisions

East Asia

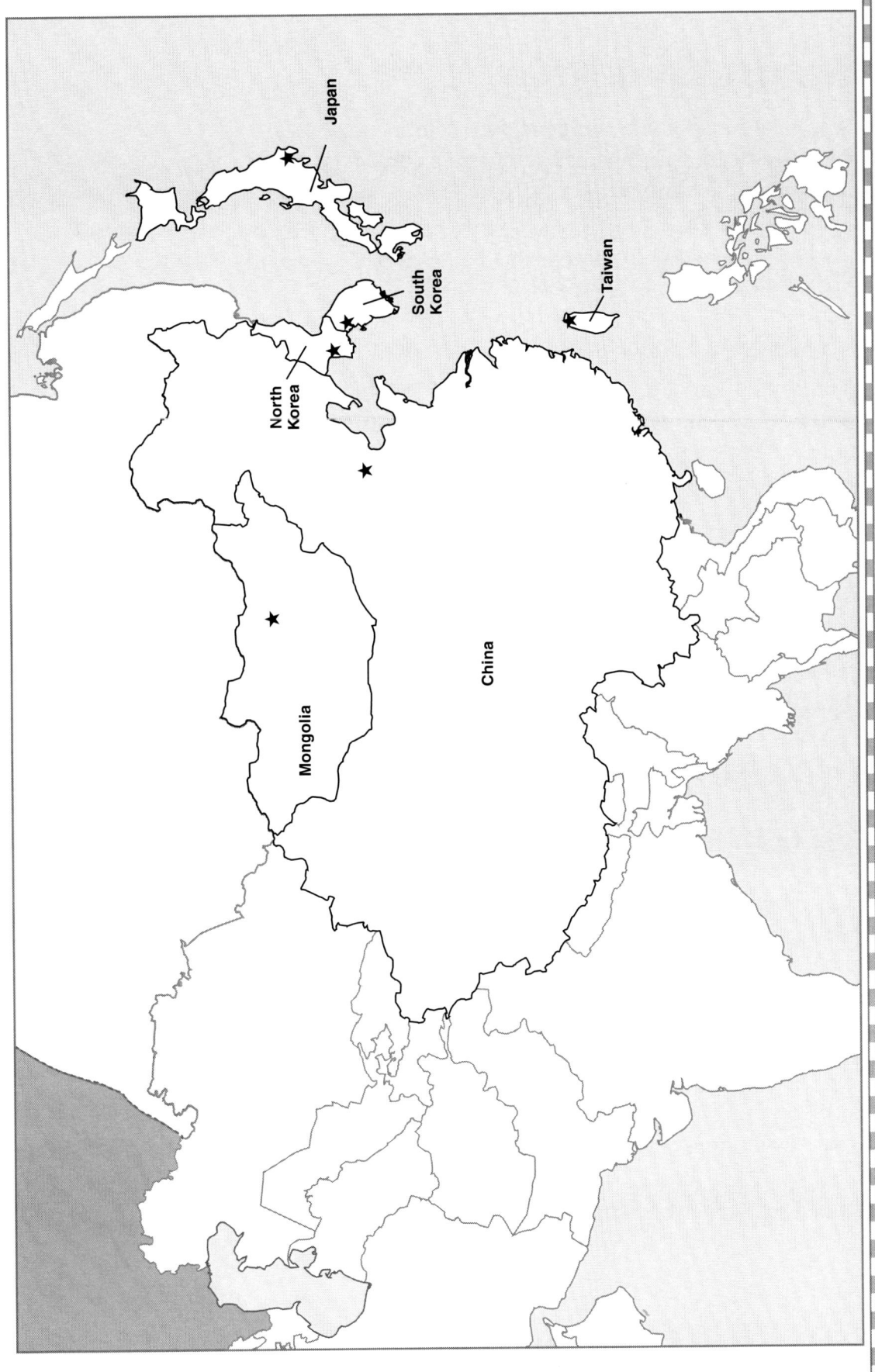

- Japan
- South Korea
- North Korea
- Taiwan
- Mongolia
- China

Name _____

www.prim-ed.com Prim-Ed Publishing

Exploring geography: Asia

Name _____

Political divisions

South-East Asia

Eleven countries make up the region of South-East Asia. They are Brunei, Cambodia, Indonesia, Laos, Malaysia, Myanmar, the Philippines, Singapore, Thailand, Timor-Leste and Vietnam. Some of the countries are located on a peninsula south of China. Others are island nations located south and east of the peninsula. The island nation of Indonesia is made up of over 17 500 islands!

The population of the region is about 539 million. Two of the largest cities are the capital cities of Jakarta, Indonesia, and Bangkok, Thailand. Jakarta has more than 9 million people, and Bangkok has more than 6 million.

Read each fact and circle the South-East Asian country that is being described. Use the information above and the map on page 39 to help you.

1. This country is made up of over 17 500 islands. **Indonesia** **Singapore**

2. Bangkok is the capital of this country. **Myanmar** **Thailand**

3. This country does *not* border the ocean. **Timor-Leste** **Laos**

4. This country is located on a peninsula. **Cambodia** **Philippines**

5. This country is the smallest in size. **Singapore** **Vietnam**

6. This island nation is east of Vietnam. **Malaysia** **Philippines**

7. Malaysia is on the same island as this country. **Brunei** **Timor-Leste**

8. This country borders the Gulf of Tonkin. **Laos** **Vietnam**

9. The Gulf of Thailand borders this country. **Indonesia** **Thailand**

10. Singapore is off the coast of this country. **Myanmar** **Malaysia**

Political divisions

South-East Asia

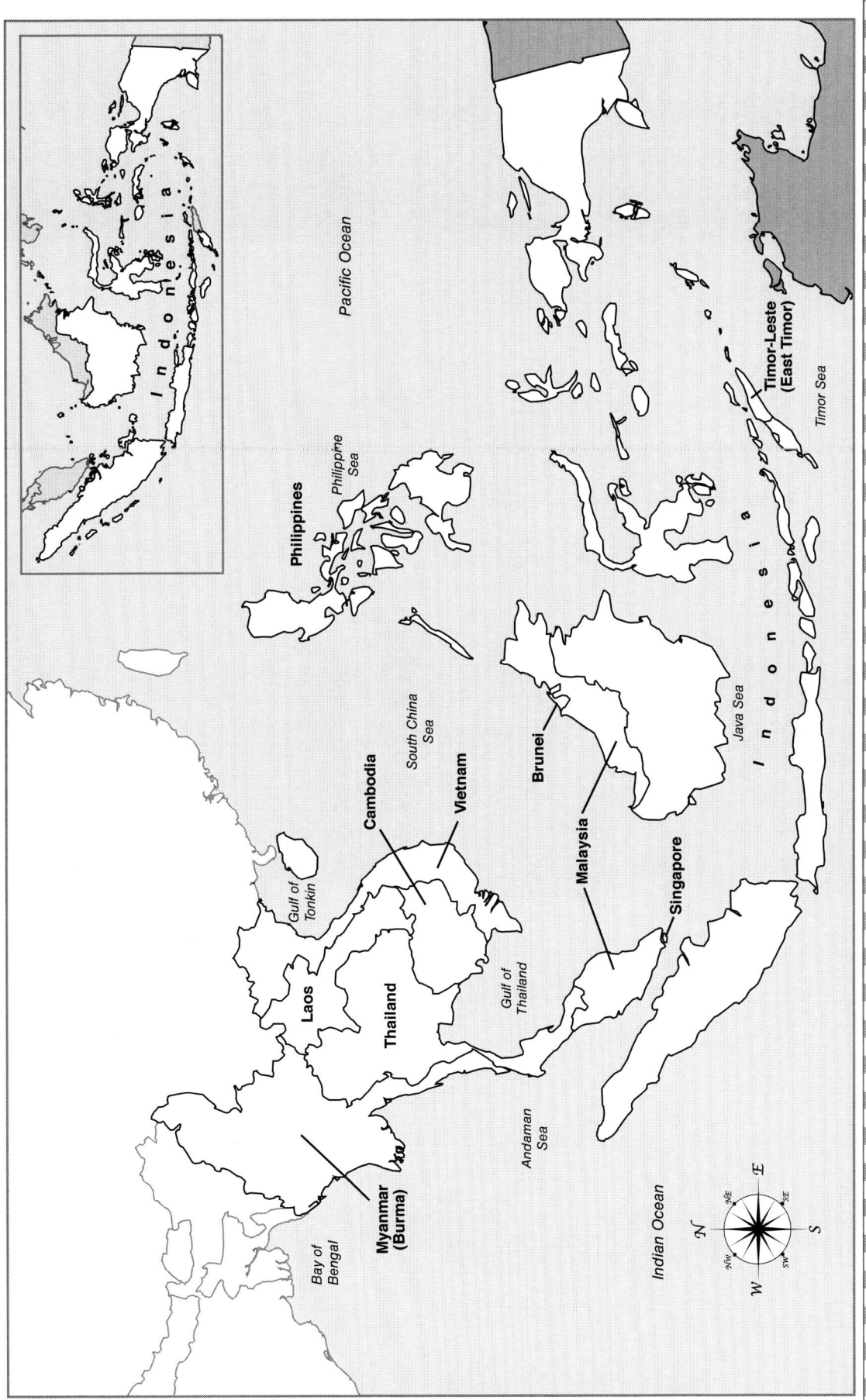

Name _____

Political divisions

Largest cities of Asia

Asia is a continent filled with densely populated cities. In fact, Asia has 14 of the 20 largest cities in the world, including the three most populated cities on Earth: Tokyo, Japan; Delhi, India; and Mumbai, India.

Most populated cities of Asia

Rank	City	Country	Population
1	Tokyo	Japan	36 507 000
2	Delhi	India	21 720 000
3	Mumbai	India	19 695 000
4	Shanghai	China	16 575 000
5	Karachi	Pakistan	13 125 000
6	Beijing	China	12 214 000
7	Tianjin	China	10 430 000
8	Istanbul	Turkey	10 378 000
9	Seoul	South Korea	9 778 000
10	Chongqing	China	9 401 000
11	Jakarta	Indonesia	9 121 000
12	Shenzhen	China	9 005 000
13	Guangzhan	China	8 884 000
14	Tehran	Iran	7 190 000
15	Hong Kong	China	7 182 000

Populations are estimates based on figures from official US Government and United Nations sources est. 2013

Name _____

Political divisions

Largest cities of Asia

A. Circle the answer to each question. Use the chart on page 40 to help you.

1. Which city has the larger population? **Mumbai**   **Delhi**

2. What is the difference in population between Jakarta and Shenzhen? **1 116 000**   **116 000**

3. In which country is Tehran located? **Iran**   **India**

4. Which city is in the top five most populated cities of Asia? **Seoul**   **Karachi**

5. How many of the top 15 cities are located in China? **seven**   **six**

6. Which city has a population of about 9.4 million? **Tianjin**   **Chongqing**

7. What is the difference in population between the largest and 15th-largest cities? **less than 10 million**   **more than 10 million**

B. New York City is the most populated city in the United States of America, with about 8 364 000 people. Use this information, as well as the chart on page 40, to answer the questions.

1. How many Asian cities have a higher population than New York City?   _____

2. How many more people does Shanghai have than New York City? Write your answer in standard form.   _____

3. Name the Asian cities in the chart that have fewer people than New York City.

_____

Review

Use words from the box to complete the crossword puzzle.

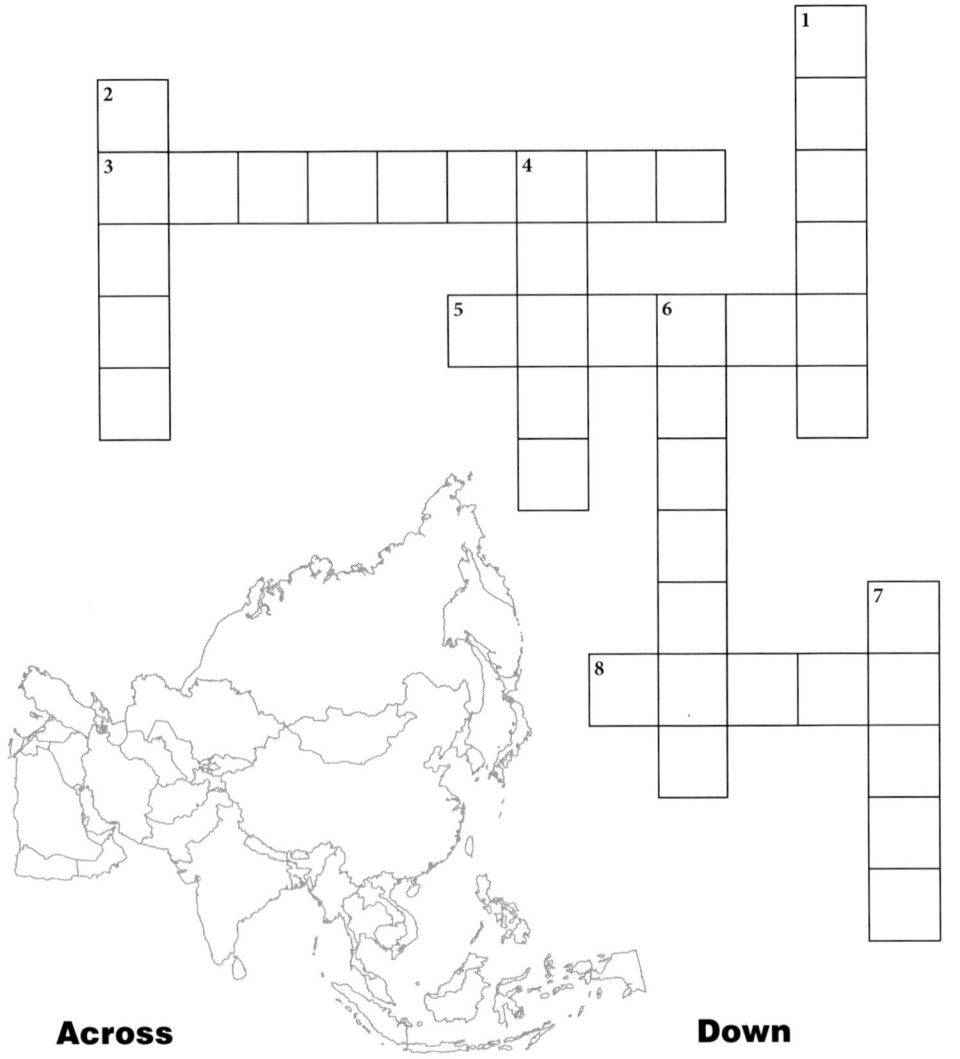

| billion |
| China |
| fifty |
| Indonesia |
| Mumbai |
| North |
| Russia |
| South |

Across

3. The country of _____ is made up of over 17 500 islands.
5. _____ is the third-largest city in Asia.
8. _____ Asia is the largest region in area, but the smallest in population.

Down

1. The largest country in area is _____.
2. Asia is made up of _____ countries.
4. India, Pakistan and Bangladesh are the largest countries in _____ Asia.
6. Asia's population is over four _____.
7. The country with the largest population is _____.

SECTION 3

Physical features of Asia

This section introduces pupils to the landforms and bodies of water of Asia. Pupils discover that Asia's landscape includes rugged mountains, dry deserts, vast plains, lush forests and thousands of islands, as well as many of the world's largest rivers, lakes and inland seas. Pupils also become familiar with the oceans, seas, bays and gulfs that surround Asia.

CONTENTS

Overview 44–45	Japan's islands 58–59
Asia's diverse landscape 46–47	Asia's tropical rainforests. . . . 60–61
The Himalayas. 48–49	Asia's bodies of water 62–63
Trek to the summit of Everest .50–51	Asia's inland seas and lakes . 64–65
The Indian subcontinent 52–53	Important rivers of Asia 66–67
The Arabian and Gobi Deserts 54–55	Review. 68
Siberia's landforms 56–57	

Name _____

Physical features

Overview

Asia is the world's largest continent. It is part of the same landmass as Europe—no body of water separates the two continents completely.

Asia has some of the world's largest and most famous landforms and bodies of water.

KEY
= Mountains
= Desert
= Water
= River

Landforms

Asia has more mountains than any other continent. The highest mountain range in the world, the Himalayas, is located in Asia. And the world's highest mountain, Mount Everest, is in the Himalayas.

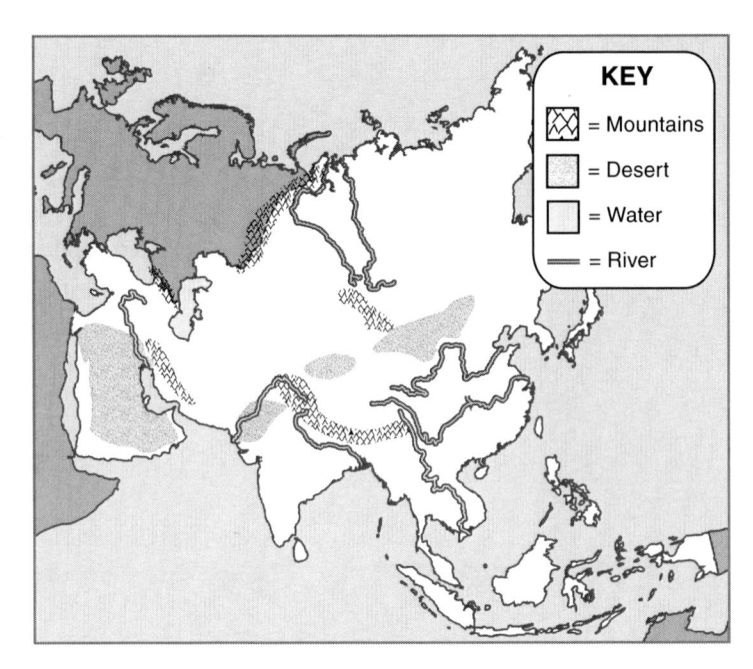

Asia also has large, barren deserts. Asia's largest desert, the Arabian Desert, is hot and sandy. The second-largest desert in Asia is the Gobi Desert, which is colder and has some grassland.

Plains and plateaus make up much of northern Asia. The West Siberian Plain is the largest level region in the world. The Central Siberian Plateau and the East Siberian Uplands also stretch across this region of Asia.

In the far east, Asia becomes a continent of thousands of islands. Japan, the Philippines and Indonesia are just three of its island nations.

Bodies of water

Asia is a continent surrounded by and filled with many large and famous bodies of water. It is bordered on three sides by the Arctic, Indian and Pacific oceans. It is also surrounded by many seas, including the Arabian Sea, Bering Sea and Red Sea.

Inland, there are several bodies of water. The Caspian Sea is the world's largest inland body of water and is actually a salt lake. The Dead Sea in the Middle East is the lowest lake on the Earth. The largest freshwater lake in the world is Lake Baikal in Russia.

Several long, winding rivers flow through Asia, including the Yangtze (Chang Jiang) River, which is the longest river in Asia. Other long rivers are the Ganges, Indus and Mekong rivers.

Name _____

Physical features

Overview

Tick the correct box to answer each question or complete each sentence.

1. Mount Everest is found in the ____.
   ☐ Ural Mountains
   ☐ Himalayas
   ☐ Arabian Desert
   ☐ Central Siberian Plateau

2. The Gobi is the second-largest ____ in Asia.
   ☐ plain
   ☐ plateau
   ☐ sea
   ☐ desert

3. Which sea does *not* border Asia?
   ☐ Arabian Sea
   ☐ Bering Sea
   ☐ Caribbean Sea
   ☐ Red Sea

4. Which statement is true?
   ☐ The Dead Sea is the lowest lake on the Earth.
   ☐ The Caspian Sea is a freshwater lake.
   ☐ Lake Baikal is actually a salt lake.
   ☐ The Arabian Sea is the world's largest inland body of water.

5. The ____, or ____, is the longest river in Asia.
   ☐ Indus, Ganges
   ☐ Ganges, Mekong
   ☐ Yangtze, Chang Jiang
   ☐ Chang Jiang, Mekong

Name _____

Physical features

Asia's diverse landscape

Much of Asia's land is rugged, meaning it has rough terrain. The continent features high mountains, grassy plains, frozen tundra and barren deserts. But Asia also has lush forests ranging from dense *coniferous*, or evergreen, forests in Russia to tropical rainforests in the South-east. With a continent this large, it's no wonder that the landscape is so diverse.

A. Look at the physical map of Asia on page 47. Use the map to answer the questions.

1. Which desert is between the Altay Mountains and the Manchurian Plain? _____

2. What is the name of the major peak shown on the map? _____

3. What kind of landform makes up the Arabian Peninsula? _____

4. Which mountain range helps form the north-western border of Asia? _____

5. What is the name of the plain that is between the Ob and Yenisei rivers? _____

6. In which direction are the Altay Mountains from the Himalayas? _____

7. Which plateau is located south of the Himalayas? _____

8. What is the name of the landform that is east of the Gobi Desert? _____

B. Read the directions to colour the map on page 47.

1. Colour the mountains brown.

2. Colour the deserts yellow.

3. Use blue to outline the rivers.

4. Use green to circle the names of the plains and plateaus.

Physical features

Asia's diverse landscape

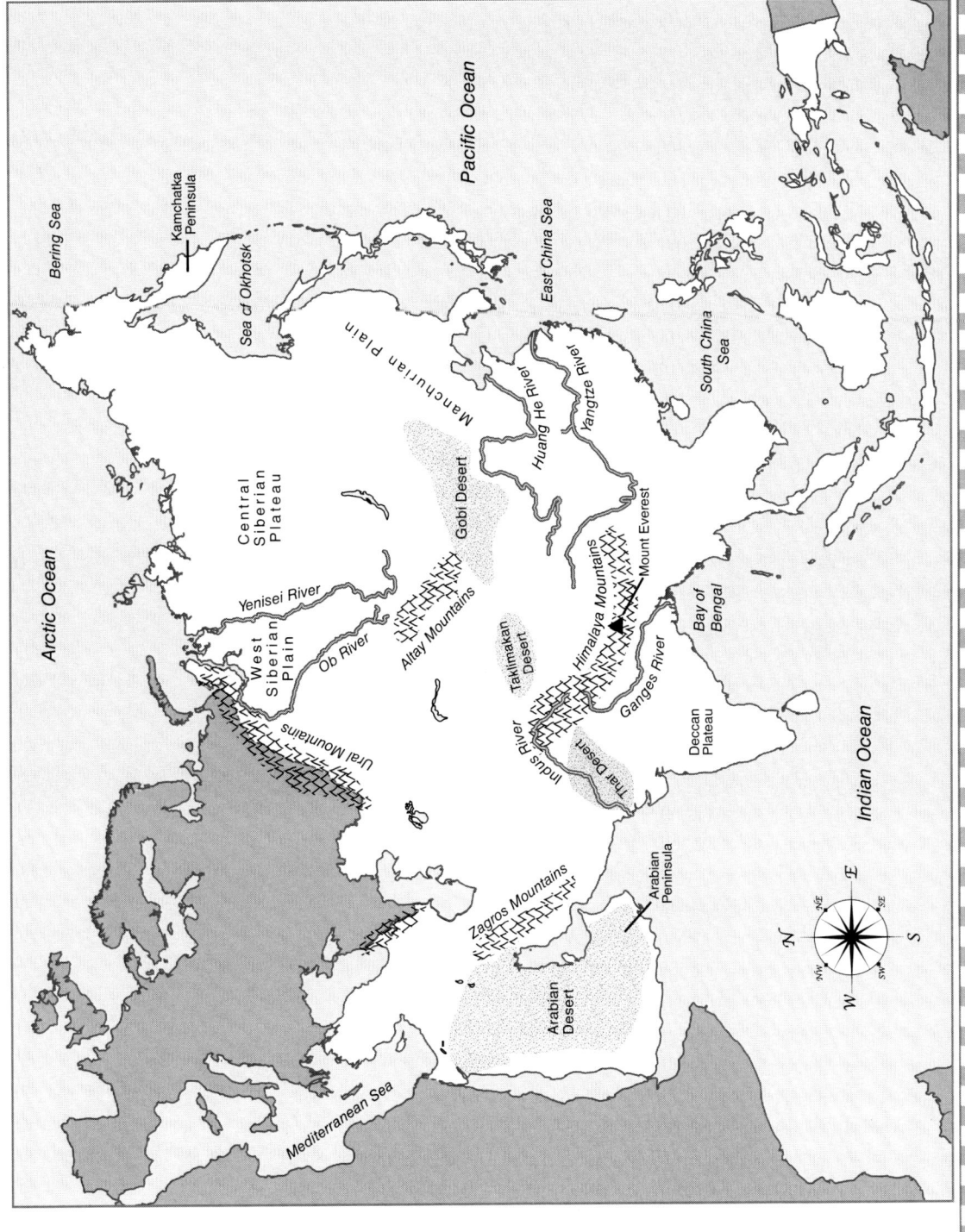

Name _____

The Himalayas

With several peaks towering above 8200 m, the Himalayas are the world's highest mountains. They lie between India and China.

Facts about the Himalayas

- *Himalaya* means 'house of snow' or 'snowy range' in Sanskrit, an ancient language of India.
- The highest peak in the Himalayas is Mount Everest, which is located on the border of Tibet and Nepal.
- The mountain system is about 2400 km in length, which makes it the third-longest system of mountains in the world.
- Five countries border the Himalayas—Bhutan, India, Nepal, Pakistan and the Tibetan part of China.
- There are about 15 000 glaciers throughout the Himalayas.
- Ten of Asia's largest rivers flow down from the Himalayas.
- Despite the harsh conditions and high elevations, the Himalayas still provide a habitat for a variety of animals, including wild yak, red pandas, snow leopards and Himalayan black bears.

There are more than 100 mountains that are over 7200 m high in the Himalayas. Below are the 10 highest peaks of the mountain range.

Highest Himalayan peaks

Rank	Mountain peak	Location	Height in metres
1	Everest	Nepal/Tibet	8850 m
2	K2	Pakistan/China	8611 m
3	Kanchenjunga	Nepal/India	8586 m
4	Lhotse	Nepal/Tibet	8516 m
5	Makalu	Nepal/Tibet	8463 m
6	Cho Oyu	Nepal/Tibet	8201 m
7	Dhaulagiri	Nepal	8167 m
8	Manaslu	Nepal	8163 m
9	Nanga Parbat	Pakistan	8126 m
10	Annapurna	Nepal	8091 m

Name _____

Physical features

The Himalayas

A. Read each statement. Circle **yes** if it is true or **no** if it is false. Use the information on page 48 to help you.

1. The Himalayas border six countries in Asia. Yes   No

2. The Himalayan mountain range is the longest in the world. Yes   No

3. Major Asian rivers flow from the Himalaya Mountains. Yes   No

4. Even though the Himalayas are snow-covered, there are no glaciers. Yes   No

5. All of the 10 highest mountain peaks are located in Nepal or Tibet. Yes   No

6. K2 is the second-highest mountain peak in the Himalayas. Yes   No

7. Mount Everest is 8611 m high. Yes   No

8. There are only 10 mountains in the Himalayas that are higher than 7200 m. Yes   No

9. Of the 10 highest mountain peaks, four of them border both Nepal and Tibet. Yes   No

10. The third-highest mountain peak is Kanchenjunga at 8586 m. Yes   No

B. Circle the correct answer under each question. Use the chart on page 48 to help you.

1. What is the difference in feet between the highest and the tenth-highest mountains in the Himalayas?

   about 800 metres   about 80 metres   about 8 metres

2. How many metres taller is Lhotse than Dhaulagiri?

   96 metres   196 metres   349 metres

Name _____

Physical features

Trek to the summit of Everest

For most mountain climbers, the ultimate experience is to climb to the *summit*, or highest point, of Mount Everest. The first trip to the summit was by Sir Edmund Hillary and Tenzing Norgay. The two men reached the top on 29 May 1953. Since then, thousands of climbers have achieved this feat and hundreds have died trying.

Every May, climbers fly into Kathmandu (kat-man-DOOH), the capital city of Nepal, to begin their expeditions. Climbing parties are usually made up of about 10 climbers and 20 Sherpa guides. Sherpas are people who live on the slopes of the Himalayas and are known for their endurance at high altitudes.

Climbers first establish a base camp near the bottom of the mountain before attempting to reach the summit. For about 30 days, the climbers will move up and down between Base Camp and four higher camps, allowing their bodies to get used to the reduced amount of oxygen in the air.

To get from Base Camp to Camp 1, climbers hike across deep crevasses of ice and snow. The most dangerous part of this climb is the Khumbu Icefall. Climbers use aluminium ladders to get across it. From Camp 1, climbers travel up through a valley called the Western Cwm (coom). Here, they get their first view of the highest peaks of Everest before reaching Camp 2, or Advanced Base Camp. To reach Camp 3, travellers must trek up a sleek wall of blue glacial ice. Fixed ropes help guide the climbers as they push upward. Before climbers get to Camp 4, they must scramble over two more obstacles—the Yellow Band and the Geneva Spur, both of which require ropes to traverse them. Oxygen tanks become a necessity at Camp 4. This area is sometimes called the 'death zone' because many climbers have died there.

Just before they get to the top, climbers face a final hurdle—the Hillary Step—a 12-metre wall of snow and ice. When the climbers reach the summit, most stay only minutes. They need to descend before nightfall, because temperatures can drop to –73 °C.

South-east Ridge Route to Everest summit

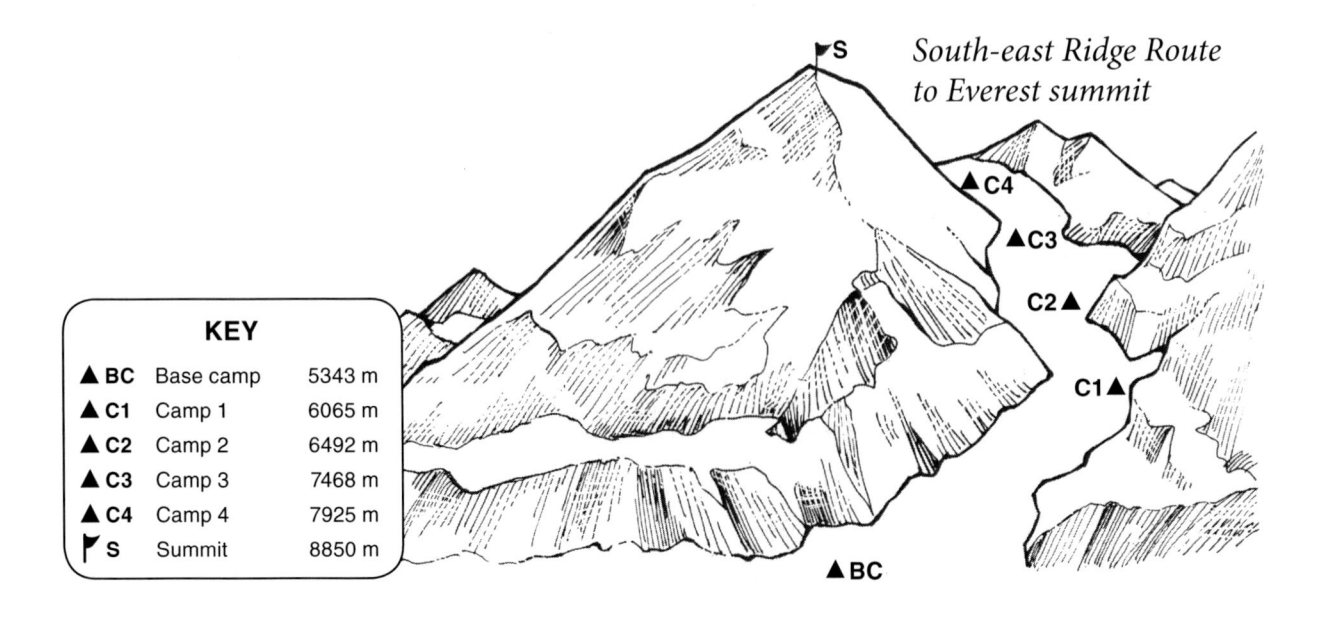

KEY		
▲ BC	Base camp	5343 m
▲ C1	Camp 1	6065 m
▲ C2	Camp 2	6492 m
▲ C3	Camp 3	7468 m
▲ C4	Camp 4	7925 m
⚑ S	Summit	8850 m

Trek to the summit of Everest

A. Look at the illustration and key on page 50 to find out the elevation of each camp along the climb to the summit of Mount Everest. Pretend you are a climber on this expedition. Write a journal entry for each point on the route.

Base camp: _____

_____

Camp 1: _____

_____

Camp 2: _____

_____

Camp 3: _____

_____

Camp 4: _____

_____

Summit: _____

_____

B. Would you like to climb Mount Everest? Explain why or why not.

_____

_____

_____

_____

Name _____

Physical features

The Indian subcontinent

About 200 million years ago, all the continents were connected. They formed a 'supercontinent' that scientists call *Pangaea*. The supercontinent was made up of plates that moved over Earth's surface at a very slow rate. Over time, the plates moved away from each other, causing the supercontinent to separate into individual landmasses. Those landmasses became the continents we know today.

One of the plates, called the Indian Plate, separated and collided with Asia 50 million years ago. The land rippled up as the two landmasses came together. The land that was pushed up became the Himalaya Mountains, with the area south of the mountains forming a large peninsula.

The continent of Asia grew bigger because of this collision. The newer part of Asia is now the region of South Asia, also known as the Indian subcontinent. A subcontinent is a large area of land that is part of a continent, but is considered a separate geographical unit. Geographers call South Asia a subcontinent because although it is big, it is isolated from the rest of Asia due to mountain ranges.

Today the Indian subcontinent consists of six countries. The country of India takes up three-quarters of the area. Bangladesh, Bhutan, Nepal, Sri Lanka and parts of Pakistan make up the rest of the large peninsula.

The Indian subcontinent

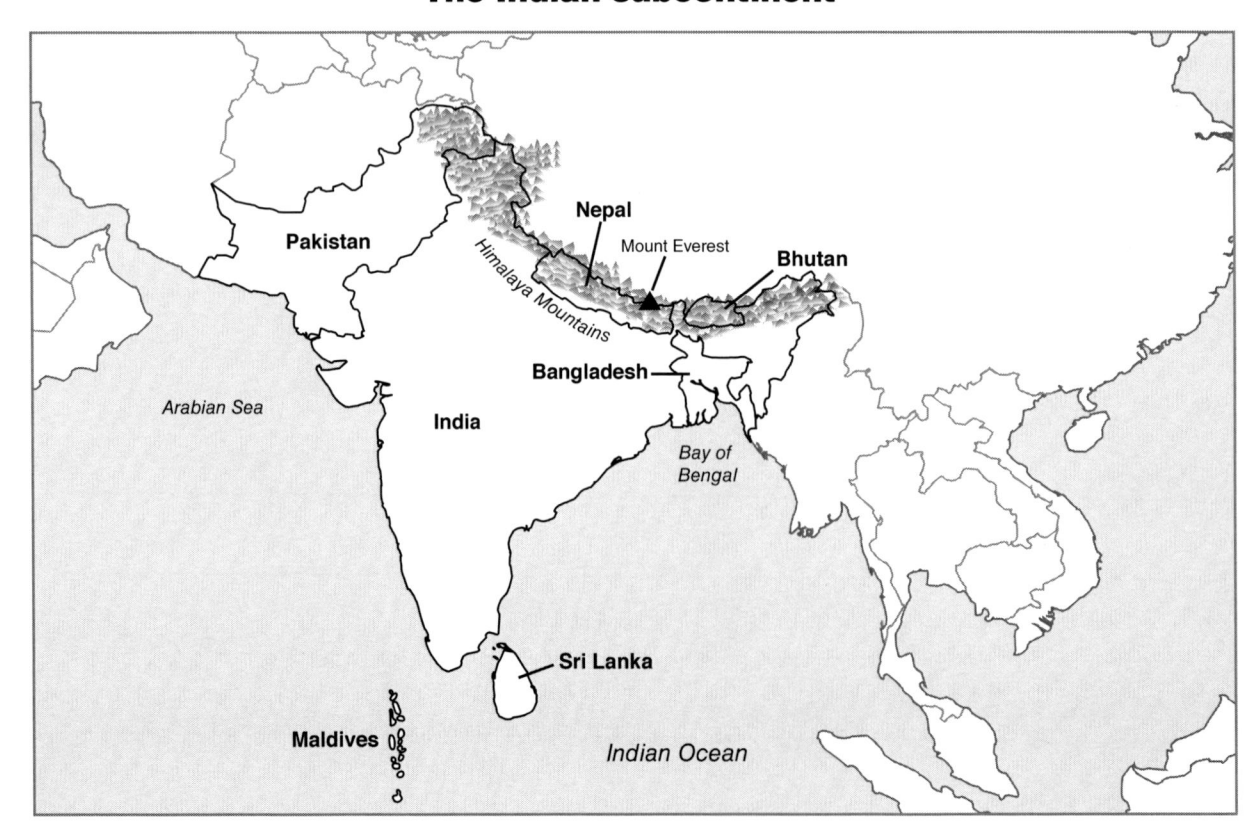

Name _____

Physical features

The Indian subcontinent

Now that you have read about the Indian subcontinent and studied the map on page 52, you are ready to complete the secret code! Read each clue and write the correct word on the numbered lines. Then use the numbers to crack the code.

1. Large bodies of ____ border the peninsula on three sides.

   __ __ __ __ __
   1 16 3 13 5

2. Pangaea eventually separated into the seven ____ we know today.

   __ __ __ __ __ __ __ __ __
   15 7 8 3 10 8 13 8 3 4

3. Most ____ say that South Asia is a subcontinent.

   __ __ __ __ __ __ __ __ __ __
   12 13 7 12 5 16 6 11 13 5 4

4. The Himalayas formed when two ____ pushed against each other.

   __ __ __ __ __ __
   6 9 16 3 13 4

5. The Indian subcontinent is a large ____.

   __ __ __ __ __ __ __ __ __
   6 13 8 10 8 4 2 9 16

6. The Indian Plate ____ with Asia 50 million years ago.

   __ __ __ __ __ __ __ __
   15 7 9 9 10 14 13 14

Crack the code!

Some people think the Indian subcontinent looks like an ____.

__ __ __ __ __ __ __ __ __
16 5 5 7 1 11 13 16 14

Name _____

Physical features

The Arabian and Gobi Deserts

The Arabian Desert

The Arabian Desert is the largest desert in Asia, covering most of the Arabian Peninsula in South-West Asia. The desert has an area of about 2.6 million square km. That's about one-third the size of Australia! Countries that lie entirely in this desert are Saudi Arabia, Kuwait, Qatar, the United Arab Emirates, Oman and Yemen. Parts of Jordan, Syria and Iraq also lie within the desert.

Most of the Arabian Desert is made up of barren highlands and plains. The northern part of the desert is a rocky plateau. Sand dunes are common throughout the entire desert. In fact, the south-east part of the desert contains the largest continuous area of sand on Earth.

Temperatures in the summer can reach 50 °C in this very hot, dry desert. The average winter temperature is 5 °C. Most of the desert receives less than 10 cm of rainfall per year.

The Gobi Desert

The Gobi Desert is the second-largest desert in Asia and stretches across parts of southern Mongolia and northern China. The Gobi has an area of more than 1.3 million square km.

The Gobi has rocky or sandy soil in the centre, surrounded by *steppes*, or dry grasslands. Unlike the Arabian Desert, sand dunes cover only 5% of the Gobi.

The Gobi is considered a cold desert. That is because it is bitterly cold at night year-round and during the winter. In the summer, temperatures can reach as high as 45 °C. But in the winter, temperatures can fall to –40 °C at night. Most of the Gobi receives less than 25 cm of rainfall per year.

Name _____

Physical features

The Arabian and Gobi Deserts

A. Use the information and maps on page 54 to complete the Venn diagram comparing the Arabian and Gobi deserts. The 'Both' section has been filled in for you.

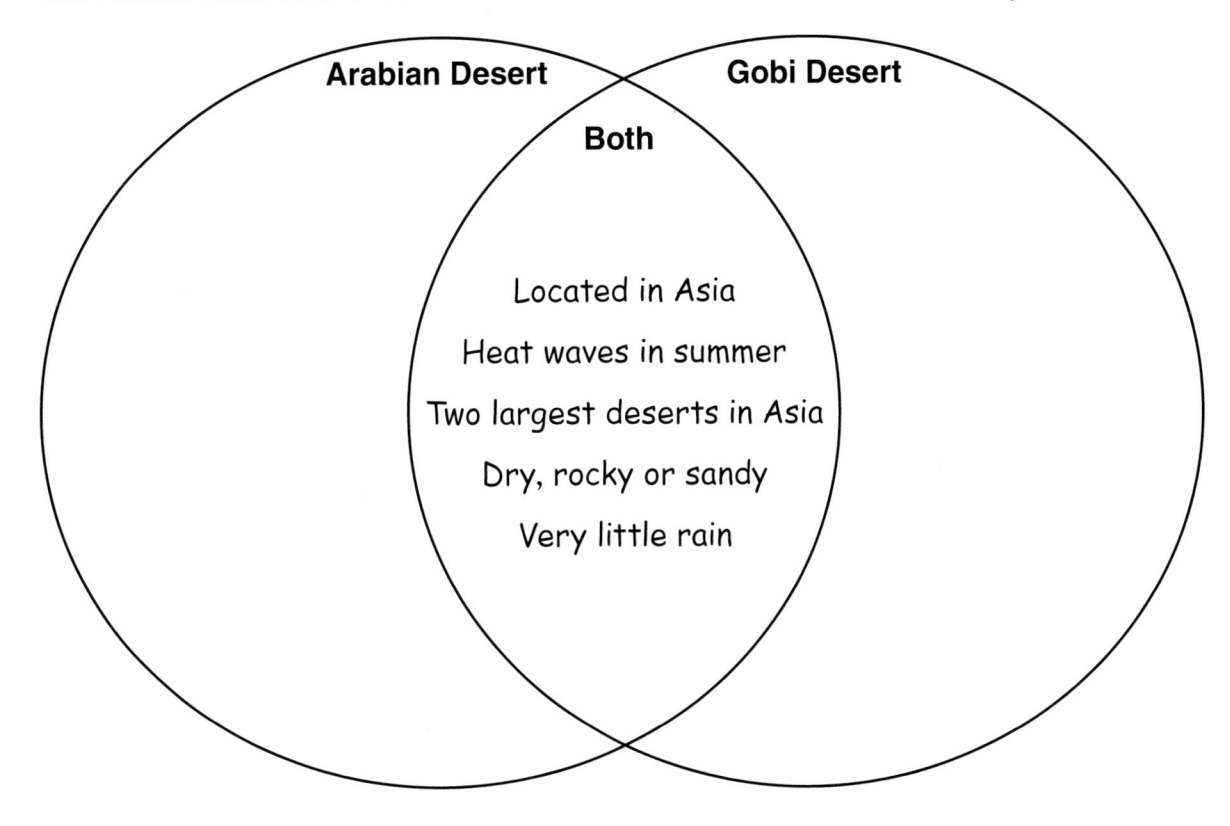

```
        Arabian Desert          Gobi Desert
                        Both

                   Located in Asia
                   Heat waves in summer
                   Two largest deserts in Asia
                   Dry, rocky or sandy
                   Very little rain
```

B. Use the information and maps on page 54 to answer the questions.

1. Name the countries that lie entirely within the Arabian Desert.

   _____

2. Name the countries that lie partly within the Gobi Desert.

   _____

3. Which desert has the coldest winters? _____

4. Which desert receives the least amount of rainfall? _____

5. Which desert has more sand dunes? _____

Name _____

Physical features

Siberia's landforms

Siberia is a huge, cold region in northern Asia. It has an area of about 12 789 000 square km and lies within the country of Russia. In fact, Siberia makes up about 75% of Russia. However, less than 20% of the Russian people live there. That is because of the region's harsh, arctic climate. In much of Siberia, extreme cold temperatures, snow and ice last for about six months of the year. The temperature in some parts can drop below −68 °C. In addition to its climate, Siberia is known for its unique landscape. The following landforms can be found in the region:

plains: large areas of flat, treeless countryside

plateaus: level areas of land that stand higher than the surrounding areas

steppes: vast, grass-covered plains rich in soil; also called *grasslands*

taiga: an evergreen forest area

tundra: an arctic area in which the top layer of soil freezes and thaws, while the second layer, called *permafrost*, stays frozen all year

uplands: elevated lands, as in hills or mountains

wetlands: a lowland area made up of marshes and swamps

A. Write the letter of the definition that matches each term. Use the information from this page to help you.

____ 1. permafrost

____ 2. plain

____ 3. plateau

____ 4. steppes

____ 5. wetlands

____ 6. taiga

____ 7. tundra

____ 8. uplands

a. a hilly area where you might find mountains

b. an arctic plain that remains frozen except for the ground just at the surface

c. grasslands that have rich soil for farming

d. an area of swampland

e. a layer of permanently frozen soil

f. a large, flat area of land

g. a cold, evergreen forest region

h. a large, mostly level area of land that stands higher than the surrounding area

Name _____

Physical features

Siberia's landforms

Physical map of Siberia

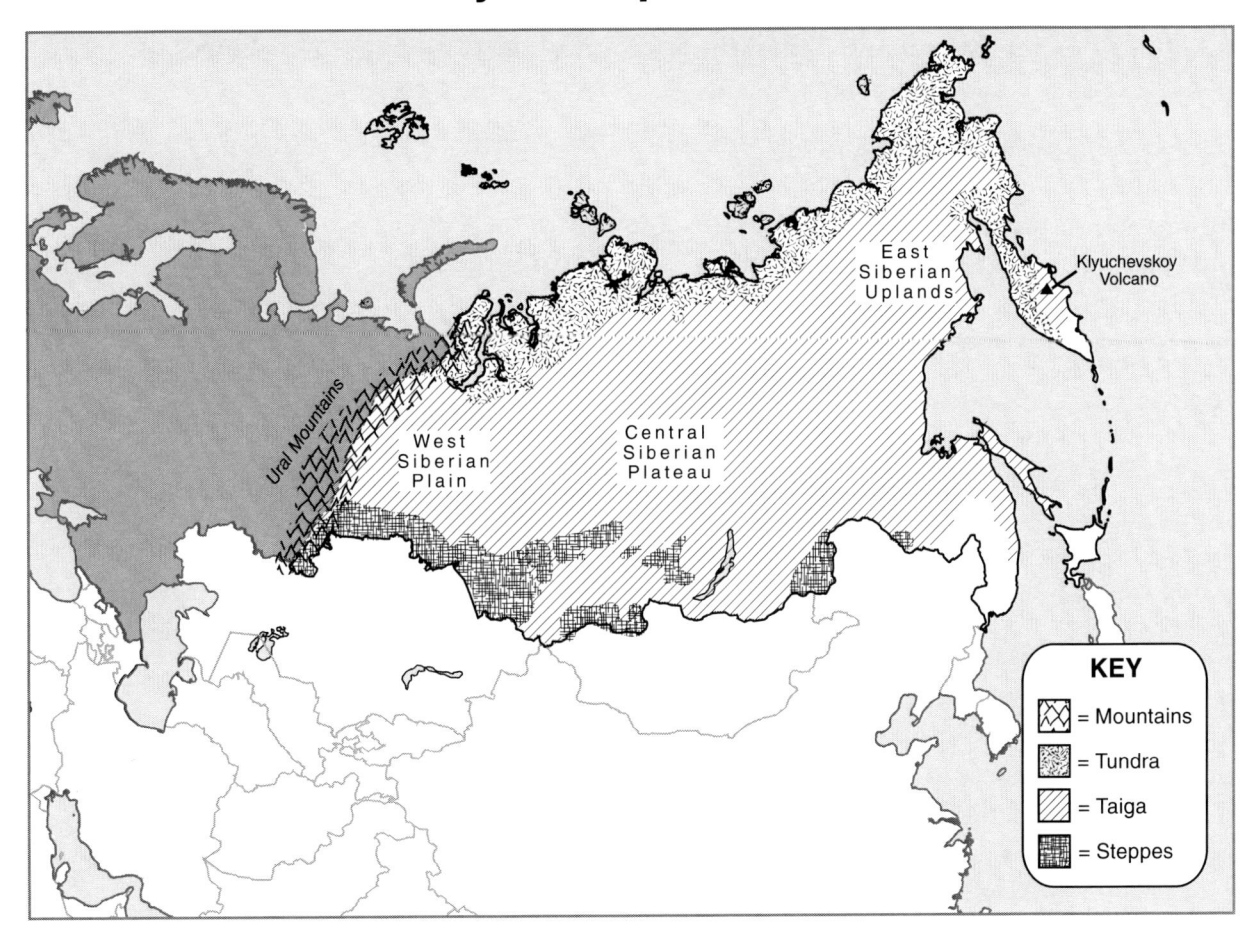

[Physical map of Siberia showing Ural Mountains, West Siberian Plain, Central Siberian Plateau, East Siberian Uplands, and Klyuchevskoy Volcano.]

KEY
- ⊠ = Mountains
- ▦ = Tundra
- ▨ = Taiga
- ▦ = Steppes

B. Write a caption for the physical map of Siberia that describes at least two of its different landforms.

_____

_____

_____

Name _____

Physical features

Japan's islands

Japan is an island country that lies off the east coast of mainland Asia. Japan is made up of an *archipelago* (ah-kuh-PEL-uh-goh), or group of islands. It has four major islands—Hokkaido, Honshu, Kyushu and Shikoku—and thousands of smaller ones. The islands form a curve that is about 1930 km long.

Japan is a land of majestic, very dangerous natural landforms, including rocky peaks, deep gorges, tall waterfalls and thick forests. Mountains and hills cover about 70% of the country. In fact, the islands are part of a great mountain range that rises from the floor of the Pacific Ocean.

Japan lies along part of the Ring of Fire, a huge area that encircles the entire Pacific Ocean where over half the world's volcanoes are found. The Japanese islands alone have more than 150 major volcanoes and over 60 of them are active. Mount Fuji, on the island of Honshu, is the highest and most famous volcanic mountain in Japan. It is 3776 m high.

About 1500 earthquakes also occur in Japan each year. Most of them are minor tremors, but severe earthquakes happen every few years. Occasionally, undersea earthquakes cause a series of huge, destructive waves called *tsunamis*, which crash along Japan's Pacific coast.

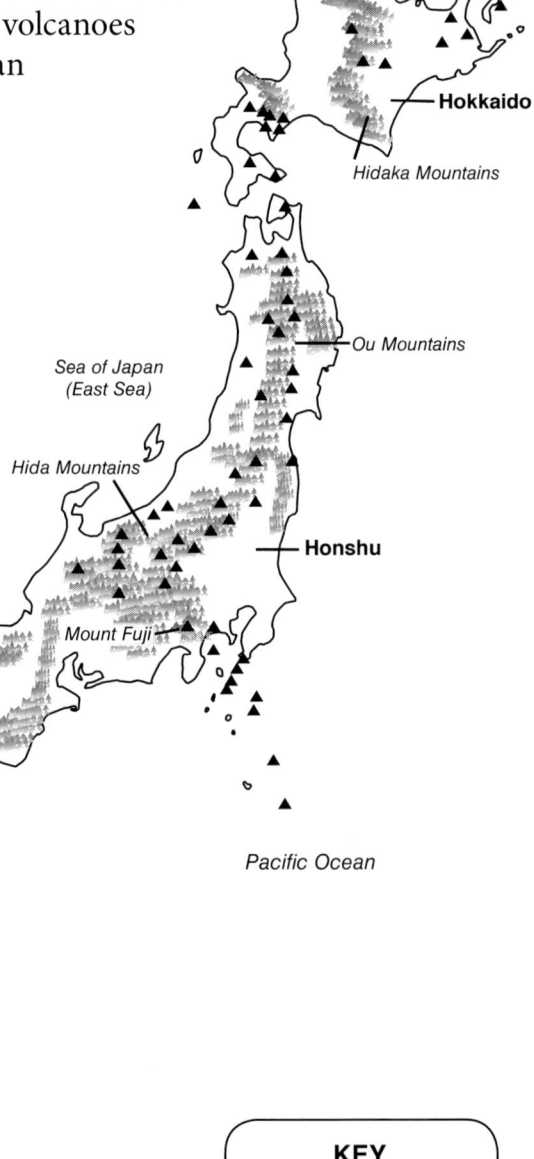

KEY

▲ = Active Volcanoes

 = Mountains

58   Exploring geography: Asia   Prim-Ed Publishing   www.prim-ed.com

Name _____

Physical features

Japan's islands

A. Use the information on page 58 to answer the questions.

One of the answers will need to start with a capital letter.

1. How many major islands does Japan have? _____

2. Which two landforms cover 70% of Japan? _____

3. What is the name and height of the highest volcanic mountain in Japan? _____

4. Of the 150 major volcanoes on Japan's islands, how many are active? _____

5. What is an *archipelago*? _____

6. Describe what can happen along Japan's coast when there is a strong undersea earthquake.

   _____

   _____

B. Write a paragraph explaining why Japan is considered a majestic, very dangerous place to live.

_____

_____

_____

_____

_____

_____

Asia's tropical rainforests

In contrast to the arctic climate of the north, South-East Asia is the continent's warm, tropical region. Rainforests grow in parts of Brunei, Cambodia, Indonesia, Laos, Malaysia, Myanmar, the Philippines, Singapore, Thailand and Vietnam, covering about 2.6 million square km of land. The South-East Asian rainforests are some of the most biologically diverse on the planet. However, people are destroying these rainforests faster than in any other tropical region. This is because there are few protected wildlife areas in South-East Asia, so there is nothing to stop people from logging and farming the land.

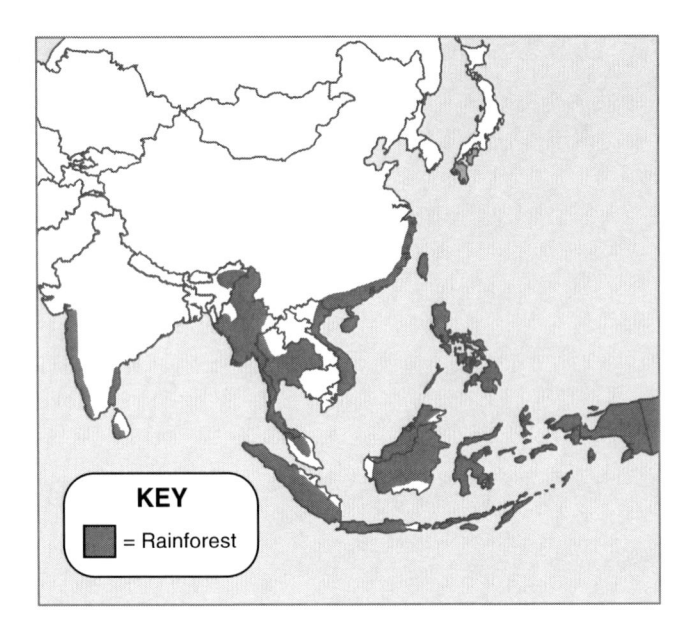

KEY
■ = Rainforest

Facts about Asian rainforests

- The South-East Asian rainforests are the oldest ones on Earth. They date back 70 million years.

- Winds called *monsoons* control much of the climate in the rainforests. The winds bring heavy rains and sometimes *typhoons*, or hurricanes. The rainforests receive 152 to 254 cm of rain each year.

- The climate is very hot and humid. Average humidity ranges from 70% to 90%. The average temperature is 27 °C in the rainforest and the highs can reach 35 °C.

- Trees grow so close together in the rainforests that falling rain often never reaches the ground.

- The *tualang* tree, a tall tree species that grows in the rainforest, can reach up to 76 m high. Bees build honeycombs that hang from its branches. The combs can be 180 cm across and contain as many as 30 000 bees.

- Two famous plants of the rainforest are pitcher plants and rafflesia. Pitcher plants are unusual because they trap and feed on insects. The rafflesia's claim to fame is that it is the world's largest flower. It is more than 91 cm wide.

- Many of the animal species that live in the rainforest, including the rhinoceros, tiger, elephant and tapir, are on the brink of extinction.

Asia's tropical rainforests

A. Complete each sentence by unscrambling the word under the line. Use the information on page 60 to help you.

1. Asian rainforests are located in a _____ region.
   aciportl

2. Winds called _____ control much of the rainforest climate.
   nomsonos

3. The climate of the rainforest is hot and _____.
   mhidu

4. The _____ tree is home to thousands of bees.
   aangtul

5. The rafflesia is the world's largest _____.
   owrelf

6. _____ and Indonesia are two countries that have rainforests.
   almyasai

7. The Asian rhino, tiger, tapir and elephant are near _____.
   citenxinot

8. The ancient rainforests of Asia have existed for 70 _____ years.
   ilomlin

B. Write three reasons why you would or would *not* like to visit an Asian rainforest.

1. _____

2. _____

3. _____

Name _____

Physical features

Asia's bodies of water

Asia has a variety of bodies of water, from frigid arctic oceans in the north to warm tropical waters in the south. It is surrounded on three sides by the Arctic, Pacific and Indian oceans. It is also bordered by several large seas. These include the Mediterranean and Arabian seas in the west, the South China and Philippine seas in the east and the Bering and East Siberian seas in the north.

With a continent so big, it's no wonder there are also many large inland bodies of water, ranging from long, winding rivers to sprawling inland seas and lakes. Famous rivers include the Ganges River in India and the Yangtze (Chang Jiang) River in China. The Caspian Sea on the western border of Asia is the world's largest inland sea. In Russia, Lake Baikal is the largest freshwater lake in the world. The Dead Sea on the border of Israel and Jordan is the lowest lake on the Earth.

A. Find and circle the bodies of water in the word puzzle. Words may appear across, down or diagonally.

```
Y D P U H C J S N H E U L U C
A E H J N A R A B I A N Q I C
N F I Y S R A S V K J T F C G
G W L A B E R I N G L I H U B
T K I Z T R H Y R I C O D Q A
Z L P U G S A C D A I F U F K
E T P L W B I A P L W L Q G I
J C I J S F C S Z U W A L A S
Y I N E Y I L P A G L A K N T
R N E U T R J I Y H K F T G E
V D W C T J W A Y I G K C E M
N I R E A R S N A E N F A S U
K A V I P N N B Z Q L D A X K
D N T S N G A O L H J Q U P Y
J P A R I B A L K H A S H S O
```

Oceans:
  Arctic
  Indian
  Pacific
Seas:
  Arabian
  Bering
  Caspian
  Philippine
Lakes:
  Baikal
  Balkhash
Rivers:
  Ganges
  Indus
  Yangtze

B. Write two facts you learned about Asia's bodies of water.

1. _____

2. _____

Physical features

Asia's bodies of water

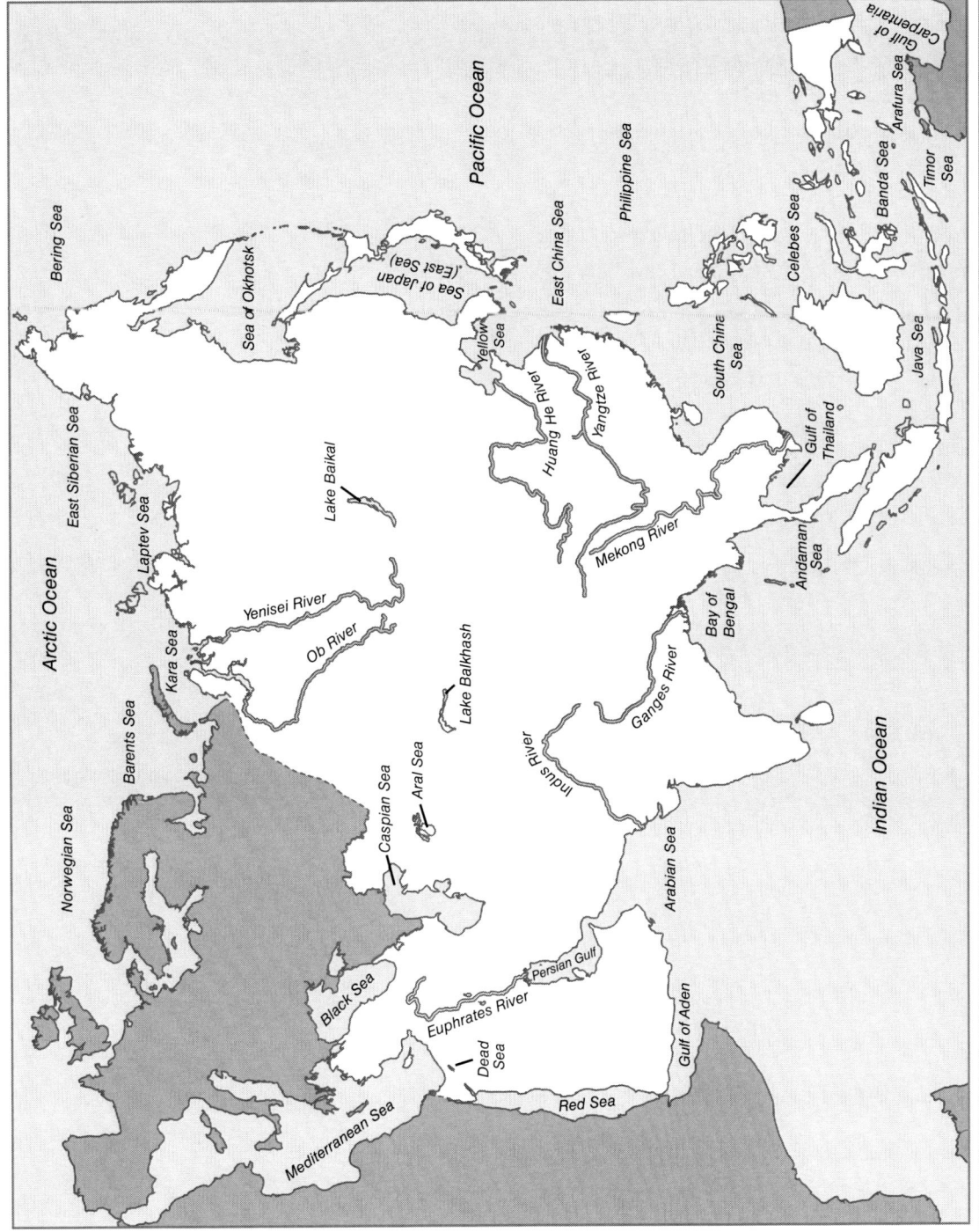

Name _____

Asia's inland seas and lakes

There are many types of seas in and around the continent of Asia. Some seas border the coast of the continent, such as the Sea of Okhotsk off the coast of Russia. But others are inland, completely surrounded by land. Inland seas are actually large saltwater or freshwater lakes. For example, the Dead Sea and the Sea of Galilee are both inland seas located in the Middle East. But the Dead Sea is a saltwater lake, while the Sea of Galilee is a freshwater lake. One lake, Lake Balkhash in Kazakhstan, has both freshwater and saltwater.

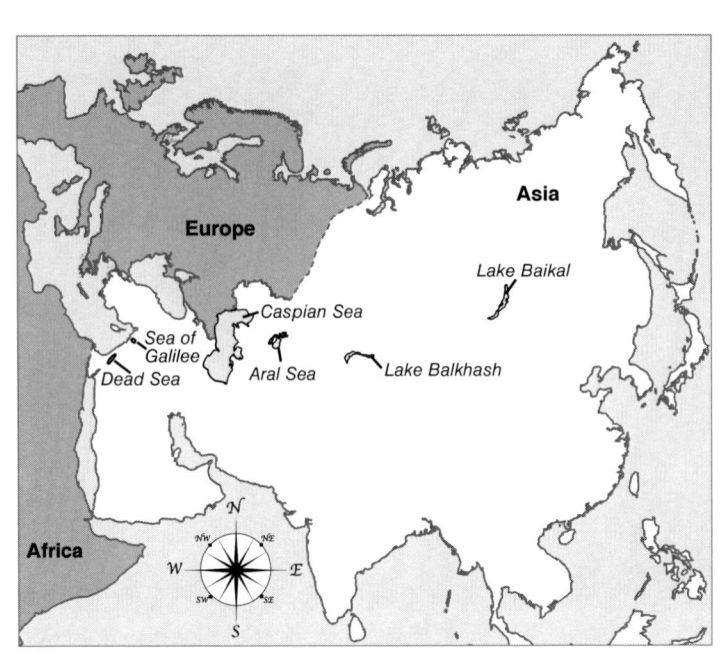

Look at the map and chart for information about some of Asia's inland seas and lakes.

Seas and lakes	Type	Location	Interesting facts
Aral Sea	saltwater	between Kazakhstan and Uzbekistan	It was once one of the world's largest inland bodies of water. Since the 1960s, the lake has shrunk to about a quarter of its former size due to the use of the water for farming.
Caspian Sea	saltwater	borders Russia, Kazakhstan, Azerbaijan, Iran, and Turkmenistan	It lies 28 m below sea level and is the world's largest inland body of water. It contains both freshwater and saltwater fish.
Dead Sea	saltwater	between Jordan and Israel	This sea lies 421 m below sea level and it is the lowest lake on the Earth. It is also the saltiest body of water in the world.
Lake Baikal	freshwater	Russia	This lake is the world's oldest lake, having formed about 25 million years ago. It is the deepest lake in the world and contains over 20% of the world's unfrozen fresh water.
Lake Balkhash	freshwater and saltwater	Kazakhstan	The western part of this lake has fresh water. The eastern part has salt water. Ice covers the lake from November to April.
Sea of Galilee	freshwater	Israel	This small freshwater lake in the Middle East is often mentioned in the Bible. The sea is also called *Lake Kinneret*.

Name _____

Physical features

Asia's inland seas and lakes

A. Circle the correct body of water. Use the information on page 64 to help you.

1. This sea is the world's largest inland body of water.	**Aral Sea**	**Caspian Sea**
2. This sea is the world's saltiest body of water.	**Dead Sea**	**Sea of Galilee**
3. This lake is the world's oldest lake.	**Lake Baikal**	**Lake Balkhash**
4. This lake has both fresh and salt water.	**Lake Baikal**	**Lake Balkhash**
5. This sea lies below sea level.	**Dead Sea**	**Sea of Galilee**
6. This sea is also called Lake Kinneret.	**Lake Balkhash**	**Sea of Galilee**
7. Since the 1960s, this sea has shrunk in size.	**Aral Sea**	**Dead Sea**
8. This sea is in the Middle East.	**Sea of Galilee**	**Lake Balkash**
9. This body of water contains over 20% of the world's unfrozen fresh water.	**Caspian Sea**	**Lake Baikal**
10. This sea is east of the Caspian Sea.	**Dead Sea**	**Aral Sea**

B. Use the chart on page 64 to answer the questions.

1. In which country is Lake Baikal located? _____

2. Which two countries share the Aral Sea? _____

3. Which lake is entirely located in Kazakhstan? _____

4. How many countries border the Caspian Sea? _____

5. The Dead Sea and Sea of Galilee share which country? _____

Name _____

Physical features

Important rivers of Asia

Asia has 32 major rivers that are over 1610 km in length. Millions of Asians live along the valleys and deltas, or areas near the mouth of the rivers. The rivers provide irrigation for farmers. They are also important transportation routes for trade and travel.

River	Length	Interesting facts
Euphrates (yooh-FRAY-teez)	2736 km	The Euphrates is the longest river in South-West Asia. The river is part of the Euphrates/Tigris river system. The world's first civilisation, Mesopotamia, developed around the Euphrates and Tigris rivers.
Ganges (GAN-jeez)	2511 km	The Ganges in India is one of the longest rivers in the world. The river plays an important part in the Hindu religion. Each year, thousands of Hindus go to the Ganges to bathe in the river and take home some of its water. Hindus believe that the water will help to purify the spirit or cure sickness.
Huang He (hwung-HAY)	5464 km	The Huang He is the second-longest river in China. The Huang He is sometimes called 'China's Sorrow' because it floods, causing much hardship for the people who live along its banks. It is also called the *Yellow River* because it carries large amounts of soft yellow earth.
Mekong (MEE-kong)	4184 km	The Mekong is the longest river in South-East Asia. It has many rapids and sandbars. No other river is home to so many species of large fish. The largest is the giant carp, which is almost 1.5 m long. Because so many dams are being built, the populations of fish are declining.
Yangtze (YANGKSEE)	6275 km	The Yangtze is the longest river in Asia and the word's third longest. It is located in China. Chinese call the Yangtze the *Chang Jiang* or *Long River*. Thousands of people live on the Yangtze. Some live and work on wooden sailboats called *junks*. The junks are used to carry food and supplies from the country to the cities.
Yenisei (yen-uh-SAY-ee)	4093 km	The Yenisei is the chief river in North Asia. It is located in the Siberian region of Russia and is frozen during the winter months. Because the upper river has so many rapids, hydroelectric stations have been built to supply energy to the region. The river is also a major transport route for lumber and grain.

Important rivers of Asia

A. Read the information in the chart on page 66. Write the name of the river to complete each sentence.

1. The _____ River is the longest river in Asia.

2. The _____ is also called the Yellow River.

3. Every year, thousands of Hindus go to the sacred _____ River.

4. The world's first civilization was built along the Tigris and

   _____ rivers.

5. Giant carp make their home in the _____ River.

6. The _____ River is 4093 km long.

7. The _____ River is located in India.

8. The _____ River is sometimes known as 'China's Sorrow'.

B. Write the names of the six rivers and their lengths in order from longest to shortest. Use the chart on page 66 to help you.

Rank	River	Length
1		
2		
3		
4		
5		
6		

Name _____

Physical features

Review

Use words from the box to complete the crossword puzzle.

Baikal
Dead
Everest
Gobi
Himalayas
Indian
Siberia
Yangtze

Across

4. The ____ subcontinent is a peninsula.
6. ____ is a region in Russia.
7. Lake ____ is the world's deepest lake.
8. Mount ____ is the highest peak in the world.

Down

1. The ____ Desert is a cold desert.
2. The ____ are the highest mountains in the world.
3. The ____ River is the longest in Asia.
5. The lowest lake on the Earth is the ____ Sea.

SECTION 4

Valuable resources of Asia

This section introduces pupils to the natural resources of Asia. Pupils discover that South-West Asia is a large oil-producing region and that China is a major producer and consumer of coal energy. Pupils also learn about Asia's main food sources—ocean fishing and rice farming. Finally, pupils explore three different kinds of forests that grow in Asia and become familiar with the wild and domesticated animals that inhabit different regions of the continent.

CONTENTS

Overview 70–71
Oil production in Asia 72–73
China's coal energy 74–75
Fishing in Asia 76–77
Rice: an Asian staple 78–79
Asia's forests 80–81
Amazing wildlife of Asia 82–85
Tigers of Asia 86–87
Working animals 88–89
Review 90

Name _____

Valuable resources

Overview

Natural resources are the minerals, plants, animals and other elements that humans use from their environment. Oil, coal, water, fish, fertile soil, forests and farm animals are examples of natural resources. The continent of Asia has all these vital natural resources.

Oil and coal

Oil is an important natural resource that is particularly plentiful in Russia and the Middle East. Countries such as Saudi Arabia, Iran and Kuwait supply a large amount of the world's oil.

Coal is another valuable resource, with China being Asia's top producer and consumer of this burnable, carbon-based material.

Fishing and farming

Ocean fishing is a big business in Asia. Many kinds of fish and shellfish from the Pacific and Indian oceans are staples of the Asian diet. Large fleets of fishing boats catch millions of tons of seafood each year to meet this demand.

About two-thirds of the people in Asia earn a living by farming. Rice is a major crop and a food staple for most Asian people. The fertile soil helps rice grow quickly. Asian farmers grow over 90% of the world's rice.

The forests of Asia

Asia has three kinds of forests. The Siberian taiga is an evergreen forest in North Asia. The North-East Asian forests are *deciduous*, or made up of trees that lose their leaves in winter. The rainforests in South-East Asia are made up of tropical trees.

Wild and domesticated animals

Asia has many unique wild animals. It is the only continent that has wild tigers. Giant pandas, orangutans and Komodo dragons are also unique to Asia.

Animals used in farming, hauling and other work include the Asian elephant, the water buffalo and the dromedary camel.

Name _____

Valuable resources

Overview

Tick the correct box to answer each question or complete each sentence.

1. Which country is the top producer of coal?
   - ☐ China
   - ☐ Russia
   - ☐ Saudi Arabia
   - ☐ Kuwait

2. ____ is a top producer of oil.
   - ☐ The Philippines
   - ☐ South-East Asia
   - ☐ The Middle East
   - ☐ Japan

3. Fish and ____ are staple foods for many Asian people.
   - ☐ meat
   - ☐ rice
   - ☐ milk
   - ☐ bread

4. The ____ is made up of evergreen trees.
   - ☐ Siberian taiga
   - ☐ South-East Asian rainforest
   - ☐ North-East Asian deciduous forest
   - ☐ none of the above

5. Which animal is used by Asian people to do work?
   - ☐ orangutan
   - ☐ giant panda
   - ☐ tiger
   - ☐ water buffalo

www.prim-ed.com Prim-Ed Publishing   Exploring geography: Asia   71

Oil production in Asia

Oil is a *fossil fuel*. This means that it was formed from the remains of animals and plants that lived millions of years ago. These remains were covered by layers of soil. Over time, heat and pressure turned the remains into what is called *crude oil*.

Crude oil is a yellowish-black liquid that is usually found in underground reservoirs. A well is drilled into the reservoir to bring the crude oil to the surface. The oil is then sent to a refinery, or factory, where it is separated into usable products such as gasoline, diesel fuel and heating oil.

Crude oil is often called 'black gold' because it is so valuable. It provides much of the world's fuel supply, it's expensive to produce and it takes so long to form that there is only a limited supply of it on Earth. Production of crude oil is an important industry in the Middle East, where huge reservoirs lie beneath Saudi Arabia, Iran and several other Middle Eastern countries. However, the single largest oil-producing country in all of Asia is Russia.

Asia's top oil-producing countries
one barrel = 159 litres

Rank	Country	Region	Barrels produced a day
1	Russia	North Asia	9 980 000
2	Saudi Arabia	Middle East	9 200 000
3	Iran	Middle East	4 700 000
4	China	East Asia	3 725 000
5	United Arab Emirates (UAE)	Middle East	2 948 000
6	Kuwait	Middle East	2 613 000
7	Iraq	Middle East	2 420 000
8	Kazakhstan	Central Asia	1 445 000
9	Qatar	Middle East	1 125 000
10	Azerbaijan	South-West Asia	1 099 000

2009 statistics from US Energy Information Administration

Name _____

Valuable resources

Oil production in Asia

A. Read each statement. Circle **yes** if it is true or **no** if it is false. Use the information on page 72 to help you.

1. Crude oil is called 'black gold' because it has gold in it.   **Yes   No**

2. Russia produces less than 9 000 000 barrels of oil per day.   **Yes   No**

3. Saudi Arabia is the top oil producer in the Middle East.   **Yes   No**

4. Kazakhstan is the only Central Asian country that produces oil.   **Yes   No**

5. China ranks third and Iran ranks fourth in oil production.   **Yes   No**

6. The country that produces the most oil per day is in North Asia.   **Yes   No**

7. Kuwait produces more oil per day than the UAE.   **Yes   No**

8. Ninth-ranked Qatar produces 1 125 000 barrels of oil per day.   **Yes   No**

9. The Middle East has six of the top 10 oil-producing countries.   **Yes   No**

10. Earth's supply of crude oil is unlimited.   **Yes   No**

B. Russia produces close to 10 000 000 barrels of oil per day. One barrel equals 159 litres. Use your maths skills to answer the questions. Circle the correct answer.

1. About how many litres of oil does Russia produce per day?

   159 000 litres   **15 900 000 litres**   **1 590 000 000 litres**

2. If oil sells for approximately $100 a barrel, how much is one day's oil production worth to Russia?

   $100 000 000   **$10 000 000 000**   **$1 000 000 000**

3. If a car uses 10 L of fuel per 100 km, and travels 20 000 km per year, about how many barrels of fuel does it use in a year?

   about 12.5 barrels   **about 20 barrels**   **about 100 barrels**

China's coal energy

Like oil, coal is a fossil fuel, but it is a solid black or brown rock that formed from decaying plant matter that has been pressed together for millions of years. Because this process takes so long, Earth has a limited supply of coal.

The main use of coal is in the production of electric power. Coal is made mostly of carbon, which can be easily lit and burned. This produces energy in the form of heat. The heat from the burning coal makes steam that drives the engines in electric power plants.

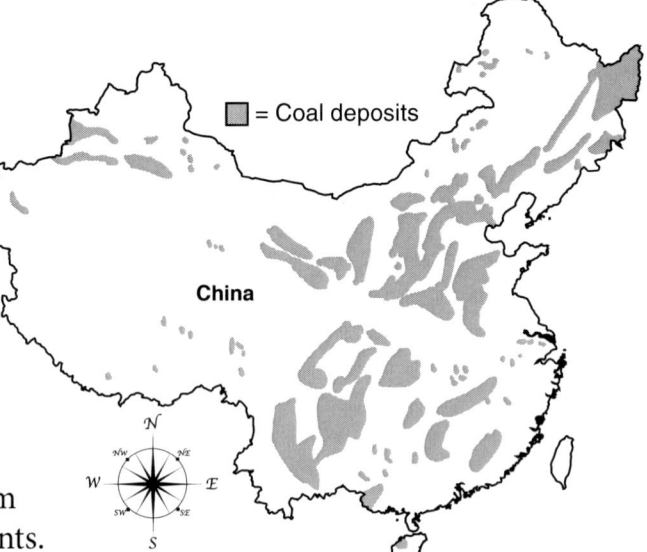

China is the world's largest producer of coal. Many parts of China have coal deposits, but the most productive coal fields are located in the north. Coal is mined, or dug up, from deep inside Earth. China has about 25 000 working coal mines.

China is also the world's largest consumer of coal, meaning it uses the most coal. The country is dependent on coal for fuel. About 70% of China's electrical energy comes from coal-burning plants.

China's coal production and use*
1980–2020

Year	Amount produced (tonnes)	Amount consumed (tonnes)
1980	684 hundred million	678 hundred million
1990	1 billion, 200 hundred million	1 billion, 100 hundred million
2000	1 billion, 300 hundred million	1 billion, 300 hundred million
2010	3 billion, 1 hundred million	1 billion, 700 hundred million
2020 projections	4 billion, 900 hundred million	2 billion, 400 hundred million

*Figures have been rounded to the nearest hundred million.
US Energy Information Administration, International Figures

Name _____

Valuable resources

China's coal energy

A. Complete each sentence by unscrambling the word under the line. Use the information on page 74 to help you.

1. Coal is a natural _____.
   ecurosre

2. China is the world's largest _____ of coal.
   cudorpre

3. Most of China's electric _____ comes from coal.
   genyer

4. In 2000, China produced and _____ about the same amount of coal.
   mesunocd

5. By 2020, almost five _____ tonnes of coal are expected to be produced in China.
   ibolnil

6. According to the chart, China produced a much _____ amount of coal in 2010 than it consumed.
   gralre

7. The heat from burning coal is used to produce _____.
   yeclritiect

8. Because coal is a form of _____, it can be easily burned.
   robcan

B. Use the map and information on page 74 to answer the questions.

1. Where are there more coal deposits in China, in the east or west? _____

2. About how many coal mines does China have? _____

3. Which part of China has the most productive coal fields? _____

Fishing in Asia

On a continent surrounded by oceans, it's no surprise that fish, shellfish and seaweed make up a large part of Asia's food supply. The countries that distribute the most of these three staples are China, Japan, Russia, Indonesia and Thailand.

Commercial fishing

Fish provides the main source of protein in the diets of millions of Asians. The Asian diet also includes shellfish such as crabs, clams, lobsters, mussels, octopuses, oysters and shrimp. To meet this need, the Asian fishing industry employs about 30 million fishermen.

Large commercial fishing vessels catch millions of tonnes of fish and shellfish each year. Japan alone brought in more than 4 million tonnes in 2007.

Fishermen use large nets that are kilometres long to catch big fish such as tuna. Shellfish are caught in baskets, boxes and other traps that are dropped into the sea.

Harvesting seaweed is also a big business. Seaweed is used not only in foods, especially in Japan, but in many medicines and beauty products.

Traditional fishing

Not all fishing is done by large fishing vessels. Small boats are used near the coastlines. Traditional fishermen in South-East Asia also depend on river fishing to provide food for their families. For example, on the Mekong River in Vietnam, Vietnamese fishermen take their catch to market in a riverboat called a *sampan*.

Fish markets

Asia is famous for its large fish markets. The largest fish market in the world, the Tsukiji Market, is in Tokyo, Japan. Here, over 400 different types of seafood are sold. Every day there is an auction to sell gigantic tuna to markets around the world.

There are also floating markets in Asia. Hundreds of workers, mostly women, pile local produce and fish into their flat-bottom boats. They float through canals on the Chao Phraya River in Bangkok, Thailand, selling their goods to families that live along the river.

Fishing in Asia

A. Find and circle the words in the word puzzle. Words may appear across, down or diagonally.

```
A F B F I S D E E J R C B A Q
B I W H S H R I M P W H K T P
M S G C H N E J L O C Z J L P
C H A L E M S A M P A N S Y I
D E I Z L V A G M E O B E X O
A R W O L H B V M C T Y A H X
U M B S F L E E T I H H W B U
O E I N I M Z I J T P S E T R
P N G A S F I B E U W I E G C
A I X L H K U K L N O I D Z E
X S F V T K R E L S L F E H O
P D C B W A Y F I S E K R V C
R A N W M X C O K P O N V H E
Y A T E V T U N A Z C O R S A
M V E H Z E G U L N U M X A N
```

- fishermen
- fleet
- market
- ocean
- sampan
- seaweed
- shellfish
- shrimp
- tuna

B. Write a sentence that gives facts about fishing in Asia. Use at least three words from the word box.

_____

_____

_____

_____

Rice: an Asian staple

Fast facts about rice

- Rice is a cereal grain. It is the chief crop of Asia.
- Asian farmers grow over 90% of the world's rice.
- More than half the world's population depends on rice as a food staple.
- There are about 250 million rice farms in Asia. Together they produce more than 575 million tonnes of rice per year.
- In some Asian languages, the word for *eat* and *eat rice* is the same.
- Rice farming in South-East Asia dates back to about 5000 BC.
- Today in South-East Asia, planting and harvesting rice is often done without machinery. Some farmers use oxen or water buffalo to pull hand ploughs.
- Most rice grows in areas of the world with a yearly rainfall of at least 100 cm.
- Rice requires an average temperature of at least 21 °C throughout its growing season in order to grow properly.
- Rice grows best in a field covered with shallow water. Asian farmers build low dirt walls called *levees* to hold water in their *paddies*, or fields.

World's top rice-growing countries

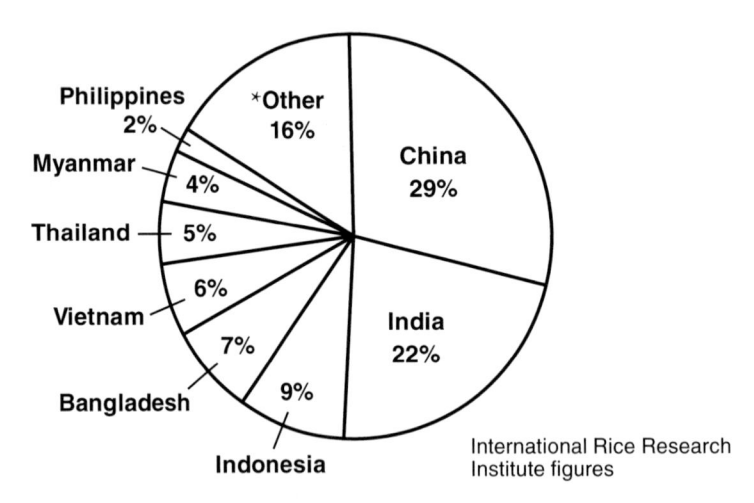

- China 29%
- India 22%
- Indonesia 9%
- Bangladesh 7%
- Vietnam 6%
- Thailand 5%
- Myanmar 4%
- Philippines 2%
- *Other 16%

International Rice Research Institute figures

* The Asian countries of Cambodia, Iran, Japan, Korea, Laos, Malaysia, Pakistan and Sri Lanka also grow rice. Each of these eight countries grows about 1% of the world's rice, or 8% of the total, while countries from other continents make up the remaining 8%.

A. Colour each section of the pie chart a different colour.

Name _____

Valuable resources

Rice: an Asian staple

B. Use the fast facts and the graph on page 78 to complete the code. Read each clue below to find each answer. Then use the numbers to crack the code!

One of the answers will need to start with a capital letter.

1. Rice is called a cereal _____.

    $\overline{}\ \overline{}\ \overline{}\ \overline{}\ \overline{}$
    9   4   14   8   6

2. Asian farmers grow over 90 _____ of the world's rice.

    $\overline{}\ \overline{}\ \overline{}\ \ \ \overline{}\ \overline{}\ \overline{}\ \overline{}$
    5   11   4   13   11   6   2

3. Most Asian rice fields are called _____.

    $\overline{}\ \overline{}\ \overline{}\ \overline{}\ \overline{}\ \overline{}\ \overline{}$
    5   14   12   12   8   11   3

4. Asian farmers depend on warm temperatures and plenty of _____ to grow rice.

    $\overline{}\ \overline{}\ \overline{}\ \overline{}\ \overline{}\ \overline{}\ \overline{}$
    4   14   8   6   10   14   7   7

5. China and _____ are the world's top producers of rice.

    $\overline{}\ \overline{}\ \overline{}\ \overline{}\ \overline{}$
    8   6   12   8   14

6. Rice fields are covered with _____.

    $\overline{}\ \overline{}\ \overline{}\ \overline{}\ \overline{}$
    15   14   2   11   4

Crack the code!

This grass, called _____, is native to North America and is not actually rice.

$\overline{}\ \overline{}\ \overline{}\ \overline{}\ \ \ \overline{}\ \overline{}\ \overline{}\ \overline{}$
15   8   7   12   4   8   13   11

Name _____

Valuable resources

Asia's forests

Forests are critical to the health of our planet. They provide homes for millions of plants and animals and they help regulate the oxygen in the atmosphere. The forests of Asia also provide their own unique resources for the people who live there. Three important kinds of forests are found in Asia.

= Taiga
= Deciduous Forests
= Rainforests

North Asia's taiga

Taiga is the Russian word for 'forest.' The Siberian taiga is the largest forest in the world. *Coniferous*, or evergreen, trees grow in the taiga. They have long, waxy needles that stay on the trees in winter. Evergreens in the taiga, including cedar, pine, spruce and fir trees, have thin trunks and grow close together. Animals such as the brown bear, moose, wolf, red fox and reindeer make their home in the taiga. Large areas of the forest are harvested for lumber and paper products.

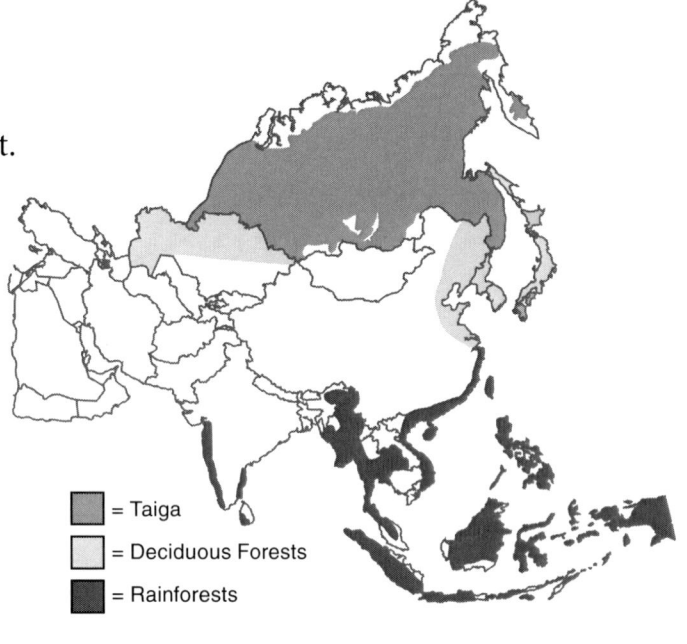

North-East Asia's deciduous forests

A deciduous forest is made up of trees that lose their leaves in winter. The North-East Asian deciduous forests cover parts of Korea, China, Russia and Japan. Common deciduous trees in this area include the elm, walnut, oak and birch. The precious Asian ginseng root is also found in the forests of North-East Asia. Asian ginseng is a gnarled root used for medicinal purposes not only in Asia, but throughout the world.

South-East Asia's rainforests

Rainforests cover about 2.6 million square km of South-East Asia. The rainforests are in India and extend eastward through Vietnam and South-east China. Rainforests are also on the islands of Indonesia, Malaysia and the Philippines. A single family of trees called the *dipterocarps* forms the rainforest canopy. The trees can reach heights of 37 m. But the tallest tree in South-East Asia's rainforests, and the third-tallest tree species in the world, is the tualang tree. It can reach heights of up to 85 m. Large honeybees make giant honeycombs in these trees and the honey is harvested by locals.

Name _____

Valuable resources

Asia's forests

A. Write the letter of the definition that matches each forest term.

____ 1. coniferous trees
____ 2. deciduous trees
____ 3. dipterocarp
____ 4. ginseng
____ 5. North Asia
____ 6. North-East Asia
____ 7. rainforest
____ 8. South-East Asia
____ 9. taiga
____ 10. tualang tree

a. a Russian word for *forest*
b. a dense tropical forest where a lot of rain falls
c. a region known for its coniferous forests
d. the third-tallest tree species in the world
e. a region known for its rainforests
f. another word for *evergreen trees*
g. a family of trees that form the canopy of a rainforest
h. a gnarled root used for medicinal purposes
i. trees that lose their leaves in winter
j. an area known for its deciduous forests

B. Write one important fact that you learned about each type of Asian forest. Use complete sentences.

North Asia's taiga: _____

_____

North-East Asia's deciduous forests: _____

_____

South-East Asia's rainforests: _____

_____

Name _____

Valuable resources

Amazing wildlife of Asia

Giant panda

The Chinese call their beloved panda a 'large bear-cat'.

Habitat
- mountain regions in central China
- lives in cool, wet bamboo forests

Characteristics
- black and white bear
- weighs up to 136 kg
- poor vision, but keen sense of smell

Diet
- eats 12.5 kg of bamboo a day
- spends 12 hours a day eating

Reproduction
- female gives birth to one or two cubs after a five-month pregnancy
- newborn cubs weigh 142 g

Behaviour
- shy, solitary animal
- skilled tree-climber and good swimmer

Enemies
- snow leopards, wild dogs
- eagles hunt panda cubs

Status
- endangered species

Orangutan

In the Malay language, 'orangutan' means 'man of the forest'.

Habitat
- rainforests of South-East Asia
- lives high in the treetops

Characteristics
- large, reddish-brown ape
- weighs up to 100 kg
- human-like thumbs for grasping

Diet
- figs, nuts, leaves, bark, insects
- gets rainwater from leaves and off its own hair

Reproduction
- female gives birth to one baby after a nine-month pregnancy
- newborn baby weighs 1 to 2 kg

Behaviour
- swings from trees, walks on four limbs
- baby clings to mother while she travels
- male roars when threatened

Enemies
- no natural predators

Status
- endangered species

Name _____

Valuable resources

Amazing wildlife of Asia

Komodo dragon

People in Indonesia call the Komodo dragon the 'land crocodile'.

Habitat
- four small islands in Indonesia
- lives in dry forests and savannas

Characteristics
- largest lizard in the world
- weighs 136 kg
- sharp claws and muscular tail
- keen eyesight and sense of smell

Diet
- carrion (dead animals), deer, goats, pigs
- has been known to kill humans
- can consume 80% of its own body weight in a single meal

Reproduction
- female lays 15 to 30 eggs
- hatchlings weigh less than 100 g and are 40 cm long

Behaviour
- solitary, territorial lizard
- can climb trees and swim

Enemies
- no natural enemies

Status
- endangered species

King cobra

The scientific name for the king cobra means 'snake eater'.

Habitat
- rainforests and plains of India, southern China, South-East Asia

Characteristics
- longest venomous snake in the world
- olive-green, tan, or black colouring with yellow crossbands

Diet
- other snakes, including venomous snakes
- lizards, frogs, small mammals
- swallows prey whole

Reproduction
- female lays 18 to 50 eggs
- young hatch in about 70 days
- the only snake that builds nests to lay eggs

Behaviour
- when threatened, raises its head off the ground and spreads its neck into a hood

Enemies
- mongoose, birds of prey such as owls and eagles

Status
- numbers declining due to loss of habitat

Amazing wildlife of Asia

Rhinoceros hornbill

Ancient people worshipped this bird as a god of war.

Habitat
- rainforests of Malaysia, Indonesia, Borneo, Java, Sumatra

Characteristics
- large black bird with white belly
- has a bony orange and red casque (horn) protruding from its head
- long beak and thick, curly eyelashes

Diet
- fruits, insects, small animals

Reproduction
- female lays one to two eggs
- birds use mud to seal female inside a tree cavity to lay her eggs
- eggs hatch in 30 days; female breaks out of cavity and reseals chicks inside for 80 days

Behaviour
- lives with mate
- makes a honking, squawking sound

Enemies
- monkeys, snakes

Status
- threatened species

Birdwing butterfly

This butterfly's official name is the Queen Alexandra's Birdwing butterfly.

Habitat
- small strip of lowland coastal rainforest in New Guinea

Characteristics
- largest butterfly in the world
- wingspan up to 30 cm
- female has brown wings, tan body
- male has blue and green markings with a bright yellow body
- poisonous if eaten

Diet
- sips nectar from the toxic pipevine plant, using its tube-like 'tongue'

Reproduction
- female lays eggs on plants
- black and red caterpillars hatch from eggs; turn into pupa
- adult butterflies emerge

Behaviour
- males chase off rivals, including birds

Enemies
- few, due to poisonous nature

Status
- very rare and endangered species

Name _____

Valuable resources

Amazing wildlife of Asia

A. Read each statement and circle the animal that is described. Use the information on pages 82–84 to help you.

1.	This animal has no natural predators.	Rhinoceros hornbill	Orangutan
2.	China is home to this shy animal.	Birdwing butterfly	Giant panda
3.	This animal is the world's largest lizard.	King cobra	Komodo dragon
4.	A casque tops the head of this animal.	Rhinoceros hornbill	King cobra
5.	When threatened, this animal stretches its neck into the shape of a hood.	King cobra	Komodo dragon
6.	This animal is rare and poisonous.	Birdwing butterfly	Orangutan
7.	This animal feeds on bamboo 12 hours a day.	Rhinoceros hornbill	Giant panda
8.	This animal eats venomous snakes.	King cobra	Orangutan
9.	The young of this animal clings to its mother while she travels.	Orangutan	Giant panda
10.	The female of this animal lays her eggs in a sealed tree cavity.	Rhinoceros hornbill	Komodo dragon

B. Which of the six animals described on pages 82–84 is your favourite? Write three reasons why.

_____

_____

_____

www.prim-ed.com Prim-Ed Publishing   Exploring geography: Asia   85

Tigers of Asia

Tigers are the largest members of the cat family. They can only be found in Asia. However, over the last 100 years, hunting and forest destruction have reduced tiger populations. Scientists think only about 3200 of these endangered animals still survive in the wild today.

At one time, eight different subspecies of tigers lived in Asia, but three became extinct in the 1900s. The five remaining subspecies are the Bengal, Indo-Chinese, Sumatran, Siberian and South China tigers. The Bengal tiger lives in the forests of India. The Indo-Chinese tiger lives in the forests of China, Thailand and Myanmar. The Sumatran tiger lives on the island of Sumatra in Indonesia. The Siberian tiger lives in the forests between Russia and China, and the South China tiger lives only in south-central China. They are the most endangered tigers in the world. There may be only 20 to 24 of them left in the wild.

Fast facts about tigers

- Most adult male tigers weigh about 180 kg. They are about 3 m long, including a 1 m tail. Females are smaller in size and weight.
- The tiger's coat ranges from brownish-yellow to orange-red and is marked by black stripes. Each tiger has a unique stripe pattern. Most tigers have yellow eyes.
- A few tigers have white coats with brown stripes and blue eyes. White tigers are extremely rare. There are about 100 white tigers and they all live in zoos.
- An adult male tiger lives alone and is very aggressive. It marks a large territory with its scent to keep other tigers away.
- A female tiger, called a *tigress*, has one to six cubs. Newborn cubs weigh only about 1 kg.
- Female cubs settle down in a territory near their mother. Males tend to roam far from their birthplace.
- Tigers hunt deer, antelope, wild cattle and wild pigs. Some may even attack young rhinos and elephants.
- A hungry tiger can eat as much as 27 kg of meat in one night.
- A tiger's roar can be heard as far as 3 km away.
- Tigers are good swimmers. They can swim across rivers and from island to island.

Name _____

Valuable resources

Tigers of Asia

A. Use the key below to colour the picture of the Bengal tiger.

KEY
White: belly, muzzle (area around mouth), chin and beard
Orange-brown: nose, face, ears, tail, paws and rest of body

B. Write a paragraph about tigers that includes at least three facts. Use the information on page 86 to help you.

_____
_____
_____
_____
_____

Name _____

Valuable resources

Working animals

Many Asian people use *domesticated*, or tamed, animals to do work. The animals are commonly called 'beasts of burden' because they carry heavy loads.

The Arabian camel

The Arabian camel is a *dromedary*, which is a camel that has one hump. The hump can store up to 36 kg of fat and allows a camel to travel up to 161 desert kilometres without water. An Arabian camel stands 2 m tall at the hump and can weigh up to 726 kg.

Arabian camels have been domesticated for almost 3500 years. They are used mostly as pack animals, meaning they carry large loads. In fact, they can carry up to 90 kg while walking 40 km a day through the hot, sandy desert. Carrying people and their goods through the vast deserts of South-West Asia has earned this camel the nickname 'ship of the desert'.

The Asian elephant

An Asian elephant is similar to an African elephant, but has differently shaped ears and is smaller. Still, the animal can weigh up to 5216 kg. The shoulder height of the Asian elephant is 3 m. Its trunk is a long nose that can grab objects. The tusks are used to dig for roots and water and to strip bark from trees.

For more than 2000 years, people have domesticated Asian elephants. They are used mostly for transportation and in the forestry business of South and South-East Asia. The elephants work in rugged country, hauling cut trees out of forests. Rangers also ride on elephants' backs, patrolling protected areas. Unfortunately, Asian elephants are endangered. Conservationists are working to save these majestic beasts.

The water buffalo

The water buffalo is a large type of cattle. The bulls, or males, are 2 m tall and can weigh from 680 to 1202 kg. Their horns can measure 4 m from tip to tip.

Water buffalo have been domesticated for more than 5000 years. There are about 153 million domesticated water buffalo in South and South-East Asia. They are used mostly for ploughing and transportation. The water buffalo, in fact, has made rice farming possible on a large scale because of its ability to plow knee-deep in mud. No wonder this giant beast is called the 'living tractor of the East'.

Name _____

Valuable resources

Working animals

A. Write a definition for each of the following terms using the information on page 88.

domesticated: _____

dromedary: _____

pack animal: _____

B. Use the information on page 88 to answer the questions.

1. What do people mean when they say camels are the 'ships of the desert'?

   _____

2. Why do people call water buffalo the 'living tractors of the East'?

   _____

C. Draw a picture of an Arabian camel, Asian elephant or water buffalo. Write a caption next to the picture. Use the information and pictures on page 88 to help you.

Review

Use words from the box to complete the crossword puzzle.

Word box:
- buffalo
- dragon
- fishing
- forest
- orangutan
- resources
- rice
- tigers

Across

1. Asians use water _____ as work animals.
5. Asian farmers grow over 90% of the world's _____.
6. _____ means 'man of the forest'.
8. The Siberian taiga is the largest _____ in the world.

Down

2. Commercial ocean _____ is a major industry.
3. The Komodo _____ is the largest lizard in the world.
4. Oil and coal are natural _____.
7. _____ are only found in Asia.

SECTION 5

Asian culture

This section introduces pupils to the architecture, education, arts, beliefs and traditions of Asia. Pupils compare different types of Asian cuisine, learn about the six major religions of Asia and study the traditions of Chinese New Year and the Japanese Doll Festival. They also discover four major tourist attractions in Asia.

CONTENTS

Overview 92–93	Education in Asia 102–103
Tourist attractions 94–95	Asian cuisine 104–105
Arts and entertainment 96–97	Celebrations 106–109
Major religions of Asia 98–101	Review 110

Name _____

Asian culture

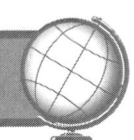

Overview

The *culture* of a group of people consists of their beliefs, customs and traditions. Culture is displayed in people's artwork, literature, language, architecture and cuisine. The rich diversity of Asia's many different cultures reflects the vastness of the continent.

Tourist attractions

Many world-famous historic and cultural tourist attractions are found in Asia, including the Taj Mahal in India, the ancient city of Petra in Jordan, the Great Wall of China and Angkor Wat in Cambodia.

Arts and entertainment

Asia has a booming arts and entertainment community. Mumbai, India, is the home of Bollywood, the world's largest film industry. In China, music, dance and martial arts are performed at the famous Beijing Opera. Japanese manga, a form of comics that are story-driven, is popular not only in Japan, but in the United States of America and Europe.

Major religions of Asia

Daily life in Asia is greatly influenced by the religious beliefs of its people. Six major religions—Buddhism, Christianity, Confucianism, Hinduism, Islam and Judaism—were founded in Asia. Christianity, Islam and Judaism began in the Middle East. Confucianism began in China and Buddhism and Hinduism originated in India.

Education in Asia

In Asia, getting a good education is very important. Although there are many rural areas that do not have access to schools or textbooks, education is stressed in most cities. Japan has one of the top education systems in the world. Primary school pupils go to school 240 days of the year. For older pupils, India has some of the best universities, colleges and technical institutes on the continent.

Asian cuisine

Popular foods such as sushi, curry and pad thai noodles originated in Asia. The diverse foods of Asia have influenced cooking all over the world.

Celebrations

Every country in Asia has its own special holidays and celebrations. Two of the most popular are Chinese New Year, which begins on the first new moon between January and February and Japan's Doll Festival, or Hina Matsuri, a day of prayer for the health and happiness of young girls.

Name _____

Asian culture

Overview

Tick the correct box to answer each question or complete each sentence.

1. Hina Matsuri is a festival held in ____.
   ☐ China
   ☐ India
   ☐ Japan
   ☐ Cambodia

2. Which of these is *not* a major religion of Asia?
   ☐ Islam
   ☐ Hina Matsuri
   ☐ Buddhism
   ☐ Hinduism

3. Which statement about education was made in the passage?
   ☐ There are no universities in India.
   ☐ Japan has one of the worst education systems on the continent.
   ☐ Pupils go to school 240 days of the year in Japan.
   ☐ Japan has the best universities in the world.

4. Which major tourist attraction is located in China?
   ☐ the Great Wall
   ☐ Petra
   ☐ the Taj Mahal
   ☐ Angkor Wat

5. Which statement is true about the culture of Asia?
   ☐ The culture of all Asian people is the same.
   ☐ Artwork, literature and cuisine are not parts of Asian culture.
   ☐ Religion is the best part of Asian culture.
   ☐ Asian culture is very diverse.

Name _____

Asian culture

Tourist attractions

Asia is a continent filled with breathtaking cultural and historic sites that draw millions of tourists each year. From amazing architecture to ancient places of wonder, Asia contains several world-famous tourist attractions.

Taj Mahal

The majestic Taj Mahal in India is a mausoleum, a type of tomb. It was built by Emperor Shah Jahan in memory of his wife, Mumtaz Mahal, who died in 1631. The Taj Mahal took 20 000 workers and 22 years to complete. Its famous dome is made of white marble and is surrounded by a 300 square metre garden with pools that reflect the building's image.

Taj Mahal

Petra

Petra is an ancient city carved into the mountains of Jordan. It was an important stop on the spice trade route and had a population of about 20 000 residents. Although most of the city's homes were destroyed in earthquakes over time, many of its rock-carved buildings still survive, including theatres and temples. Petra was even featured in the 1989 film *Indiana Jones and the last crusade*.

a building in Petra

The Great Wall of China

When the Great Wall was first built more than 2000 years ago, it was a series of separate walls constructed by different states. The Great Wall as we know it today was completed during the Ming Dynasty (1368–1644 AD) and stretches 8850 km through China.

Great Wall of China

Angkor Wat

Built in the 12th century in Cambodia, Angkor Wat was built as a Hindu temple and later became a Buddhist temple. Every year, it draws hundreds of thousands of tourists, who marvel at its architecture and the elaborate religious and historical scenes that decorate its walls. The temple is so famous that its image is featured on the Cambodian flag.

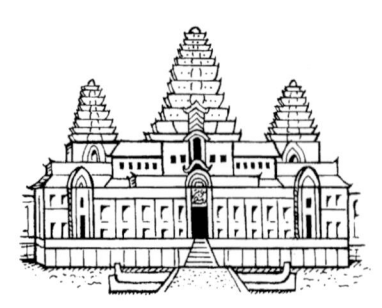

Angkor Wat

Asian culture

Tourist attractions

A. Use the information on page 94 to help you answer the questions.

1. In approximately what year was the Taj Mahal completed?

2. What architectural feature makes the ancient city of Petra unique?

3. How long is the Great Wall of China?

4. Which attraction is featured on the Cambodian flag?

5. Which place was featured in the film *Indiana Jones and the last crusade*?

6. Why did Emperor Shah Jahan build the Taj Mahal?

7. What kind of temple was Angkor Wat originally?

8. About how long ago was the Great Wall first built?

B. Which tourist attraction would you most like to visit? Explain your answer.

Name _____

Asian culture

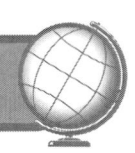

Arts and entertainment

Art is more than just drawing or painting. It can be any kind of creative expression, such as dance, literature, music and theatre. All of these art forms, and many others, flourish in Asia. Asian art, in fact, has inspired artists and performers across the globe and its influence can be seen in films, TV shows, fashion and more.

Bollywood

The largest film industry in the world is not Hollywood in the United States of America. It's Bollywood, based in Mumbai, India. The name *Bollywood* is a cross of *Bombay* (the former name of the city of Mumbai) and *Hollywood*. More than 700 films are produced in Bollywood each year, most of them musicals. Each film features elaborate song-and-dance routines, with colourful costumes and sets. Actors lip-sync the words to prerecorded songs performed by professional singers. The dances are a combination of classical Indian and folk dance with modern Western styles.

Japanese Manga

Manga, a type of comic, is extremely popular in Japan. The Japanese word *manga* means 'whimsical pictures'. The comics feature black-and-white drawings of often fantastical characters. Manga drawings are accompanied by long stories that focus on the characters' struggles. The comics can sometimes run as long as 400 pages! Manga is not just for kids. There are categories of Manga for teens and adults, as well as manga geared specifically to girls. Many animated films and TV shows are based on manga comics.

The Beijing Opera

The Beijing Opera is one of China's national treasures. Performed at the Liyuan Theatre, this spectacular cultural event involves actors and singers wearing colourful costumes and elaborate makeup. Acrobats, jesters and storytellers present dramatic plays with singing, dancing and martial arts. The productions are based on legendary tales of historic events.

performers of the Beijing Opera

Name _____

Asian culture

Arts and entertainment

A. Read each statement. Circle **yes** if it is true or **no** if it is false.

1. Martial arts can be a part of a Beijing Opera performance. — Yes   No
2. Manga is a type of Japanese comic. — Yes   No
3. Manga stories are quite short. — Yes   No
4. In Bollywood films, actors sing their own songs. — Yes   No
5. Beijing Opera productions are based on historic events. — Yes   No
6. For something to be considered art, it must be drawn or painted. — Yes   No
7. The name *Bollywood* is a combination of *Hollywood* and the former name for *Mumbai*. — Yes   No
8. Colourful costumes are a feature of both the Beijing Opera and Bollywood films. — Yes   No
9. Manga artists draw mostly ordinary characters. — Yes   No
10. Bollywood films are mostly musicals. — Yes   No
11. The Liyuan Theatre is in Japan. — Yes   No
12. Manga comics are brightly coloured. — Yes   No

B. Which would you most like to do—go to the Beijing Opera, see a Bollywood film, or read a manga comic book? Why?

_____

_____

_____

www.prim-ed.com   Prim-Ed Publishing   Exploring geography: Asia   97

Name _____

Asian culture

Major religions of Asia

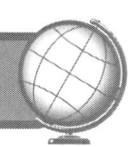

Most of the world's major religions began in Asia. Buddhism and Hinduism were founded in India and Confucianism developed in China. Christianity, Islam and Judaism all came from the Middle East region of Asia. Christianity and Judaism began in the area that is now Israel, while Islam started in what is now called Saudi Arabia.

Daily life in Asia is strongly influenced by people's religious beliefs.

The Dharma Wheel symbolizes Buddha's teachings of the path to enlightenment.

The cross is a symbol that reminds Christians that Jesus died on the cross.

Buddhism

Origin: India, 2500 years ago

Leader: Siddhartha Gautama, known as Buddha, the Enlightened One

Teachings: Followers devote their lives to finding release from suffering. They try to live a balanced life without extremes. The ultimate goal is to reach a state of peace and happiness called *nirvana*.

Sacred book: the Tripitaka

Places of worship: temples and homes

Major festival: Wesak, the celebration of Buddha's life

Followers: 300 million worldwide

Asian countries where practised most: Cambodia, Laos, Mongolia, Myanmar, North Korea, Singapore, Sri Lanka, Thailand and Vietnam

Christianity

Origin: Israel, 2000 years ago

Leader: Jesus of Nazareth, known as Jesus Christ, the Anointed One

Teachings: Followers believe in one God. They believe that God sent Jesus to save all people from sin and that people who believe in God and show love and forgiveness will go to heaven.

Sacred book: the Bible

Places of worship: churches, chapels and cathedrals

Major festivals: Christmas and Easter

Followers: 2.2 billion worldwide

Asian countries where practised most: Armenia, Cyprus, Georgia, Lebanon, the Philippines and Russia; spreading quickly in China

Name _____

Asian culture

Major religions of Asia

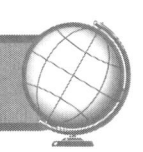

The Chinese character for water represents the religion of Confucianism.

The star and crescent symbol is commonly used to represent Islam.

Confucianism

Origin: China, 2500 years ago

Leader: Kong Qiu, known as Confucius, Great Master Kong

Teachings: Followers believe in a code of living that includes goodwill, duty, manners, wisdom and trustworthiness. They believe that the success of society depends on good and honest leaders. They do not believe in a god or an afterlife.

Sacred book: a collection of Confucius's sayings and conversations called the Analects

Places of worship: temples

Major festival: Teacher's Day on Confucius's birthday, 28 September

Followers: 350 million worldwide

Asian countries where practised most: China, Japan, Korea, Taiwan and Vietnam

Islam

Origin: Mecca (Saudi Arabia), 1500 years ago

Leader: Prophet Muhammad, known as the Praised One

Teachings: Followers (known as Muslims) believe in one God—Allah. They also believe in five pillars: faith in Allah; prayer five times a day; fasting throughout Ramadan; charity; and travel to Mecca, the holy city, at least once in a lifetime.

Sacred book: Qur'an (or Koran)

Places of worship: mosques

Major festival: Ramadan, the holy month when Muslims do not eat or drink from sunrise to sunset

Followers: 1.2 billion worldwide

Asian countries where practised most: Afghanistan, Azerbaijan, Bahrain, Bangladesh, Indonesia, Iran, Iraq, Jordan, Kuwait, Malaysia, Pakistan, Qatar, Saudi Arabia, Turkey, United Arab Emirates, Uzbekistan and Yemen

Major religions of Asia

'Om' or 'aum' is the main symbol of Hinduism. The symbol represents the sound heard in deepest meditation.

The Star of David represents the religion of Judaism. The symbol is featured on the Israeli flag.

Hinduism

Origin: India, 5000 years ago; world's oldest religion

Leader: There is no single authority. The religion grew gradually over time.

Teachings: Followers have a wide variety of beliefs. Many Hindus believe in one or more gods, such as Brahma, Vishnu and Shiva. They also believe in reincarnation, in which human and animal spirits come back to Earth in different forms to live again. There is also a belief in *karma*, the idea that a person's actions in a past life determine his or her destiny.

Sacred book: the Vedas

Places of worship: temples

Major festivals: More than 1000 important festivals each year, celebrating nature's cycle and the gods

Followers: 900 million worldwide

Asian countries where practised most: India and Nepal

Judaism

Origin: the area now called Israel, 3700 years ago

Leaders: Abraham, Jacob and the prophet Moses

Teachings: Followers believe in one God. Their beliefs are based on laws for conduct and worship, including the Ten Commandments which God revealed to Moses. These laws emphasise justice, charity, honesty and being true to one God.

Sacred book: the Torah

Places of worship: synagogues, also called temples

Major festivals: Rosh Hashanah, Yom Kippur and Passover

Followers: 12 million worldwide

Asian country where practised most: Israel

Name _____

Asian culture

Major religions of Asia

A. Find and circle the words in the word puzzle. Words may appear across, down, or diagonally.

```
A B B F I S D E E J R C B A C
B E W I S L A M B P T H K T O
M A G C B N E J L O O Z J L N
C R A L U M T N A P R A S Y F
H E I Z D V A G K E A B E X U
R H I N D U I S M A H Y I H C
I S B S H L E M T I R H R B I
S I I N I M A I J T P M S T A
T T B A S R I B N U S I A G N
I I L L M K U K L I O I S Z I
A S E R T K R E A S L F E H S
N D C U W A Y D I S E K U V M
I A G W M X U O K P O N V H E
T L T E V J U N A C O O R S A
Y V E H Z E M U S L I M X A D
```

- Bible
- Buddhism
- Christianity
- Confucianism
- Hinduism
- Islam
- Judaism
- karma
- Muslim
- Torah

B. Draw one of the religious symbols from pages 98–100. Write the religion it represents below the drawing. Then write three facts about that religion.

1. _____

2. _____

3. _____

Name _____

Asian culture

Education in Asia

Education in Asia varies greatly from place to place. Many rural areas have little access to organised schools or school materials such as textbooks. In some places, it is hard for girls and women to find educational opportunities. But in most urban areas, education is thriving. Japan and India both have some of the best education systems in Asia.

Primary school education in Japan

School is hard in Japan, where the literacy rate (people's ability to read and write) is high compared to many countries of the world. In Japan, pupils have six years of primary school, three years of middle school and three years of high school.

There are 20 to 30 pupils in a class. The main subjects taught in the fourth, fifth and sixth years are Japanese language, maths, science, geography, history, music, art and physical education. In Japanese classes, pupils learn to read and write 1006 *kanji* characters (Chinese characters used in Japanese writing). They also take classes in home economics—basic cooking and sewing—and ethics. Ethics class includes manners, respect for elders and good behaviour.

The average number of days in the school year is 240. Pupils go to school for about seven hours a day and take five or six classes each day. Each class is 45 minutes long. The pupils stay in one room for most subjects and teachers move from room to room. There are short 5- to 10-minute breaks after each class. Lunch is about 40 minutes long and there is one 20-minute break.

Classes are divided into small teams for special activities. Each week, teams clean the classrooms, halls and playgrounds of their school. They tend to the plants in and around the school. Teams also take turns serving lunch to their classmates. Two hours a week are devoted to events such as sports, cultural festivals, field trips and club meetings.

Higher education in India

In India, *higher education*, or college, begins when students are about 18 years old and have completed primary, secondary and senior secondary education levels. At that point, students may enter one of the more than 17 000 universities, colleges and technical institutes in India.

Completing higher education can take anywhere from three to five years, depending on whether students want to earn a bachelor's degree in arts or science, or a degree in engineering, medicine or law.

India is well-known for its top-notch technical institutes. At these schools, students can earn degrees in computer application, business administration, pharmacy and hotel management.

Name _____

Asian culture

Education in Asia

Fill in the chart, comparing your school or class with a typical school in Japan.

	Japan	Your school or class
Length of school year and school day	240 days, 7 hours a day	
Subjects	maths, geography, history, science, health, Japanese language, art, music, PE, home economics, moral education	
Lunch and break	Lunch is 40 minutes long and is usually eaten in the classroom. Pupils take turns serving other classmates. There is also a 20-minute break.	
Special activities during the week	cleaning the school, tending to plants, field trips, sports, festivals and club meetings	
Homework	every night and during holiday time	
After-school activities	clubs such as baseball, table tennis, chess, origami, computer lab and English lessons	

Name _____

Asian culture

Asian cuisine

Many types of food dishes that might be familiar to you come from Asia. From spicy sauces to sweet desserts, Asian cuisine is as diverse as its different cultures.

Food	Description	Origins
Sushi	raw slices of fish, such as tuna, salmon, or yellow tail, placed over sticky rice or rolled in seaweed	Japan
Kimchi	pickled vegetables with spicy seasonings	Korea
Pad thai	stir-fried noodles with egg, lime juice, peanuts, bean sprouts and shrimp or chicken	Thailand
Peking duck	roasted and seasoned duck, often served with a sweet bean sauce	China
Curry	a spicy sauce made of seasonings such as turmeric, coriander, cumin, ginger, garlic and chillies; usually served over meat and rice	India; eaten throughout South-East Asia
Baklava	sweet, flaky pastry filled with crushed nuts and covered in honey	*Turkey; eaten throughout the Middle East
Hummus	a dip made of mashed chickpeas, sesame paste, olive oil, lemon juice, garlic, salt and pepper	the Levant, an area that includes Syria, Lebanon, Israel, Jordan and parts of Turkey and Palestine
Roti canai	flatbread that is typically pulled apart and eaten with the hands	Malaysia

*Not everyone agrees on the origins of baklava, but most evidence suggests that it comes from the former Ottoman Empire in Turkey.

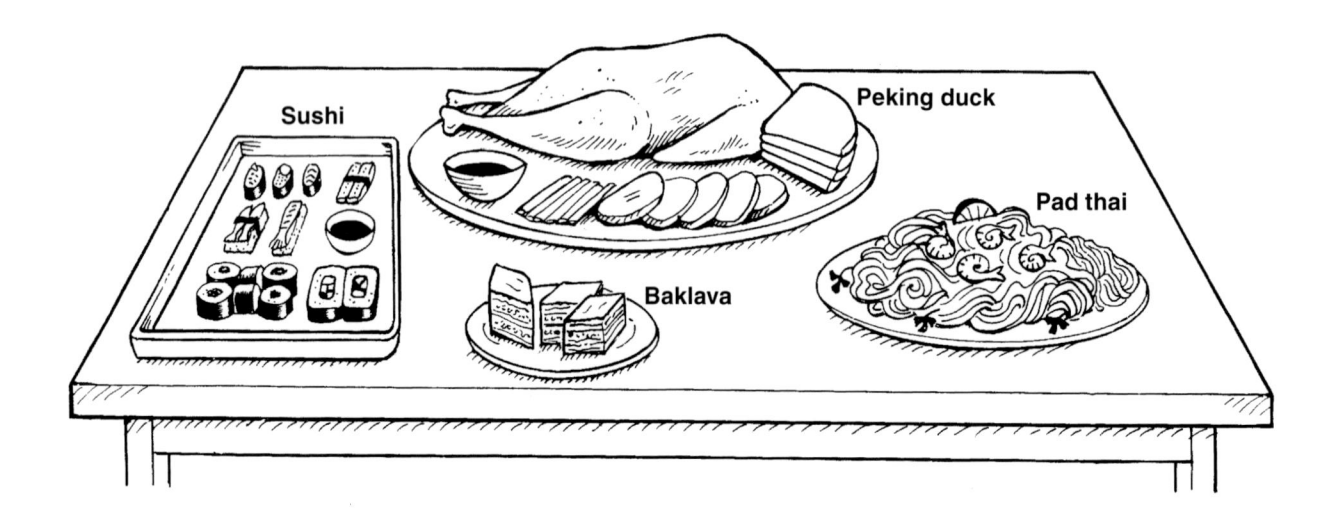

Name _____

Asian culture

Asian cuisine

A. Write the letter of the place that each type of Asian food comes from.

____ 1. sushi   a. Turkey

____ 2. curry   b. Korea

____ 3. kimchi   c. Thailand

____ 4. Peking duck   d. Japan

____ 5. roti canai   e. China

____ 6. baklava   f. the Levant

____ 7. pad thai   g. India

____ 8. hummus   h. Malaysia

B. Answer the questions.

1. Have you eaten any of the Asian foods listed on page 104? If so, which ones have you eaten?

   _____

   _____

2. If you answered 'yes' to question 1, which food was your favourite and why?

   _____

   _____

3. If you answered 'no' to question 1, which Asian food would you most like to try? Why?

   _____

   _____

Name _____

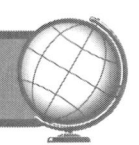

Asian culture

Celebrations

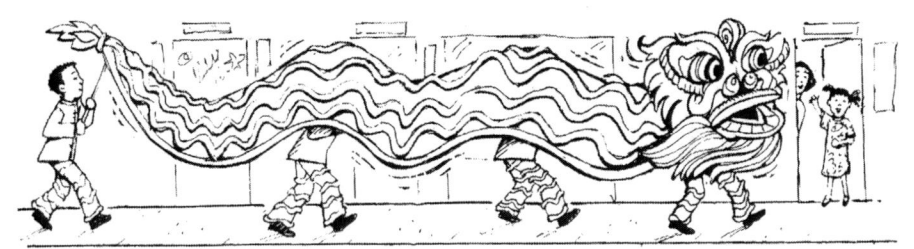

Chinese New Year

Chinese New Year is a 15-day celebration that marks the start of the new year on the Chinese calendar. The date of the festival is based on the phases of the moon. It begins on a new moon between January 21 and February 20 and ends on the first full moon 15 days later. Throughout the festival, there are parades, fireworks and dances featuring colourful lion and dragon costumes.

The following traditions are practised by many Chinese people to celebrate the beginning of the new year:

Before the festival

The home is thoroughly cleaned to sweep out the old year. Then people decorate the home. Flowers, representing rebirth and new growth, are placed throughout the house. Platters of fresh and dried sweet fruit are set out for guests. Poetic messages are written on red paper and hung on walls and doors. For example, a message might say, 'May you enjoy continuous good health'.

New Year's Eve

On the night before the first day of the festival, families gather for a special dinner. Places are set for absent family members. Many dishes of food are served, including chicken, fish, rice, spring rolls, dumplings and vegetables. Guests bring small gifts of oranges and tangerines, symbolising happiness.

New Year's Day

On the first day of the festival, families pay respects to their ancestors at local temples. People visit relatives, neighbours and friends to exchange good wishes. Children receive red envelopes filled with money to wish them good luck and wealth in the new year.

The Lantern Festival

The Lantern Festival is held on the last day of the Chinese New Year celebration and represents hope for the coming year. Lit lanterns are hung outside of homes, with riddles attached to them. Visitors who solve the riddles receive small gifts. Visitors are also given rice dumplings, which symbolise harmony and happiness. Hundreds of colourful, animal-shaped lanterns are also displayed in public areas and children carry lanterns through the streets.

Name _____

Asian culture

Celebrations

Chinese New Year

According to the Chinese calendar, each new year represents one of 12 animal signs. These animals repeat in a 12-year cycle. For example, 2013 was the Year of the Snake.

The Year of the Snake will occur again in 2025, 2037 and so on. It is said that a person born in the year of a certain animal has some of the same traits as that animal. The animal signs, their personality traits and the years they occur are shown in a chart called the Chinese Zodiac.

Read the Chinese Zodiac and circle your sign. Does it describe your personality?

The Chinese Zodiac

Tiger 1986, 1998, 2010, 2022	Rabbit 1987, 1999, 2011, 2023	Dragon 1988, 2000, 2012, 2024	Snake 1989, 2001, 2013, 2025
Brave, smart and a strong leader. Likes Horse and Dog. Beware of Monkey!	Happy, loving and a good peacemaker. Likes Sheep and Pig. Beware of Rooster!	Lucky, honest and a great adventurer. Likes Monkey and Rat. Beware of Dog!	Quiet, thoughtful and a terrific organiser. Likes Rooster and Ox. Beware of Pig!
Horse 1978, 1990, 2002, 2014	**Sheep*** 1979, 1991, 2003, 2015	**Monkey** 1980, 1992, 2004, 2016	**Rooster** 1981, 1993, 2005, 2017
Shy, cheerful and a hard worker. Likes Tiger and Dog. Beware of Rat!	Wise, generous and a talented artist. Likes Pig and Rabbit. Beware of Ox!	Clever, intelligent and funny. Likes Dragon and Rat. Beware of Tiger!	Proud, alert and a good public speaker. Likes Snake and Ox. Beware of Rabbit!
Dog 1982, 1994, 2006, 2018	**Pig** 1983, 1995, 2007, 2019	**Rat** 1984, 1996, 2008, 2020	**Ox** 1985, 1997, 2009, 2021
Dependable, honest, and a loyal friend. Likes Horse and Tiger. Beware of Dragon!	Kind, sincere and a thoughtful teacher. Likes Rabbit and Sheep. Beware of Snake!	Charming, eager and a fine inventor. Likes Dragon and Monkey. Beware of Horse!	Strong, calm and a good listener. Likes Snake and Rooster. Beware of Sheep!

*Year of the Sheep is sometimes called Year of the Goat

Name _____

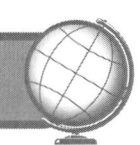

Asian culture

Celebrations

Hina Matsuri

In Japan, 3 March is the holiday of Hina Matsuri, also known as the Japanese Doll Festival. Hina Matsuri is a day of prayer for the health and happiness of young girls. Families with daughters celebrate this day by setting up a display of dolls inside the house and serving diamond-shaped rice cakes and tiny crackers.

The practice of setting up dolls began as a way to ward off evil spirits. In some parts of Japan, people still throw paper dolls into a river, hoping that the dolls will carry away sickness or misfortune.

Most people display their doll collection in the middle of February and put it away as soon as Hina Matsuri is over. This is because of an old superstition that says if families are too slow in putting away their dolls, their daughters will have trouble marrying!

The dolls of Hina Matsuri are dressed in the costumes of the Japanese imperial court, which was at its peak from 794–1192 AD. The dolls are placed on a platform that has several *tiers*, or levels, covered in red cloth. Traditionally, people put the dolls in a specific place on each tier, though many families are beginning to change or limit the doll displays because they are very expensive.

First tier

The emperor and empress sit at the top on the first tier. They sit in front of a gold folding screen, just like the real imperial throne of ancient Japan.

Second tier

Three court ladies sit on the second tier, holding small cups for *sake* (SAHKEE), a rice wine.

Third tier

Five male musicians—three drummers, a flute player, and a singer—are on the third tier.

Fourth tier

Two ministers, or counsellors of the emperor and empress, are displayed on the fourth tier. They sit on either end of a set of tables with small bowls of crackers and cakes.

Fifth tier

The fifth tier holds three servants who protect the emperor and empress.

Celebrations

Hina Matsuri

Colour the drawing of the five-tiered Hina doll set. Then write the names of the dolls that appear on each tier next to the numbers below.

Tier 1: _____

Tier 2: _____

Tier 3: _____

Tier 4: _____

Tier 5: _____

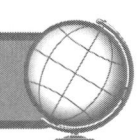

Review

Use words from the box to complete the crossword puzzle.

calendar
culture
Hina Matsuri
India
Japan
Petra
religions
Thailand

Across

2. The school year in _____ lasts 240 days.
4. Pad thai is a famous dish in _____.
6. Asia is home to six major _____.
8. _____ is the languages, beliefs, arts and traditions of a group of people.

Down

1. The Chinese _____ is based on the phases of the moon.
3. _____ is an ancient city in Jordan.
5. _____ is the Japanese Doll Festival.
7. The Bollywood film industry in _____ is the largest in the world.

Section 6

Assessment

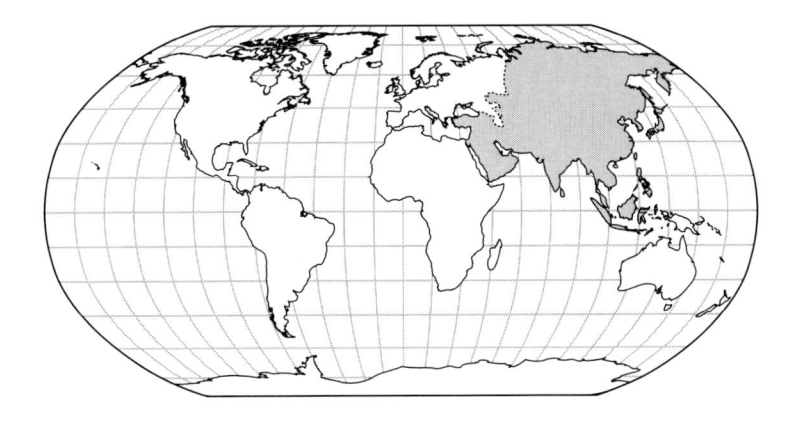

This section provides two cumulative assessments that you can use to evaluate pupils' acquisition of the information presented in this book. The first assessment requires pupils to identify selected cities, countries, landforms and bodies of water on a combined physical and political map of Asia. The second assessment is a two-page multiple-choice test covering information from all sections of the book. Use one or both assessments as culminating activities for your class's study of Asia.

CONTENTS

Map test.................... 112   Multiple-choice test...... 113–114

Name _____

Assessment

Map test

Write the name of the country, city, landform or body of water that matches each number. Use the names in the box to help you.

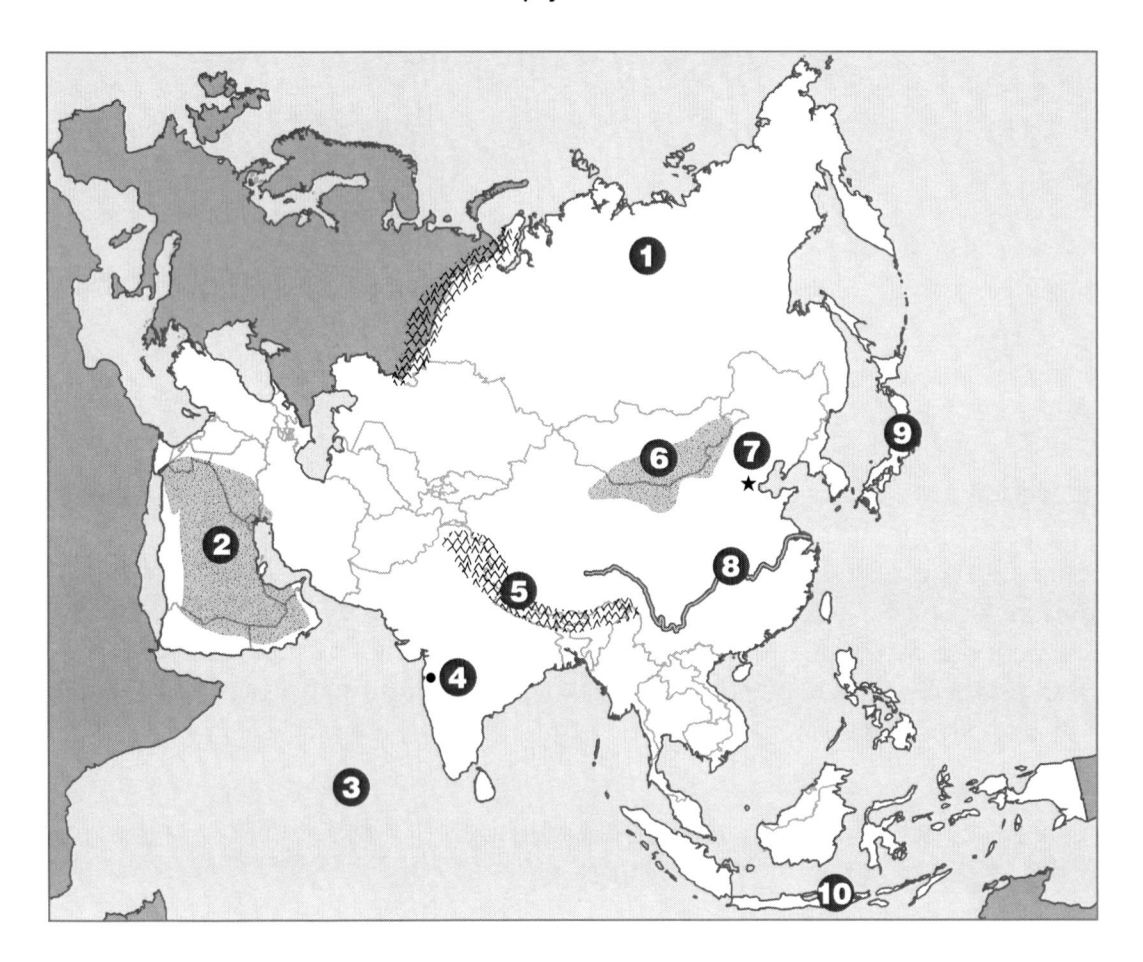

| Arabian Desert | Indian Ocean | Russia | Mumbai | Himalayas |
| Yangtze River | Gobi Desert | Japan | Beijing | Indonesia |

1. _____
2. _____
3. _____
4. _____
5. _____
6. _____
7. _____
8. _____
9. _____
10. _____

Multiple-choice test

Tick the correct box answer each question or complete each sentence.

1. Asia is the largest continent in the world in ____.
   - [ ] size
   - [ ] population
   - [ ] both size and population
   - [ ] number of cities and countries

2. Which continent shares a land border with Asia?
   - [ ] Europe
   - [ ] Australia
   - [ ] North America
   - [ ] South America

3. In which two hemispheres is Asia mostly located?
   - [ ] Northern and Southern
   - [ ] Eastern and Western
   - [ ] Southern and Western
   - [ ] Northern and Eastern

4. Asia's ____ countries are divided into ____ regions.
   - [ ] 20, 4
   - [ ] 50, 6
   - [ ] 50, 8
   - [ ] 75, 10

5. Which country is the largest in size, but smallest in population?
   - [ ] Qatar
   - [ ] Nepal
   - [ ] Russia
   - [ ] Philippines

6. Which two countries rank first and second in population?
   - [ ] China and India
   - [ ] China and Japan
   - [ ] Indonesia and Pakistan
   - [ ] Bangladesh and Vietnam

7. Which mountain range is the highest in Asia and in the world?
   - [ ] Mount Everest
   - [ ] Altai Mountains
   - [ ] Zagros Mountains
   - [ ] Himalaya Mountains

8. The ____ Desert is the largest in Asia.
   - [ ] Gobi
   - [ ] Thar
   - [ ] Arabian
   - [ ] Taklimakan

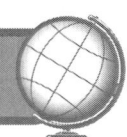

Multiple-choice test

9. Which ocean does *not* border the continent of Asia?
   - [ ] Atlantic
   - [ ] Arctic
   - [ ] Indian
   - [ ] Pacific

10. The top two oil-producing countries in Asia are ____.
    - [ ] Iran and China
    - [ ] Iraq and Kuwait
    - [ ] Qatar and Kazakhstan
    - [ ] Russia and Saudi Arabia

11. Asian farmers grow over ____% of the world's rice.
    - [ ] 20
    - [ ] 50
    - [ ] 90
    - [ ] 100

12. Which of these animals can only be found in the Asian rainforest?
    - [ ] orangutan
    - [ ] king cobra
    - [ ] giant panda
    - [ ] komodo dragon

13. Why are camels, elephants and water buffalo called *beasts of burden*?
    - [ ] They are wild animals.
    - [ ] They carry heavy loads.
    - [ ] They are endangered.
    - [ ] They work in the desert.

14. Which religion was founded in India?
    - [ ] Islam
    - [ ] Judaism
    - [ ] Hinduism
    - [ ] Confucianism

15. The date of the Chinese New Year is based on the ____.
    - [ ] phases of the sun
    - [ ] Chinese Zodiac
    - [ ] Lantern Festival
    - [ ] phases of the moon

16. A major tourist attraction in Cambodia is ____.
    - [ ] Angkor Wat
    - [ ] the Taj Mahal
    - [ ] the Great Wall
    - [ ] Petra

Section 7

Note-takers

This section provides four note-taker forms that give pupils the opportunity to culminate their study of Asia by doing independent research on places or animals of their choice. (Some suggested topics are given below.) Pupils may use printed reference materials or internet websites to gather information on their topics. A cover page is also provided so that pupils may create a booklet of note-takers and any other reproducible pages from the book that you would like pupils to save.

FORMS

Physical feature 116

Suggested topics:

- Annapurna Mountain
- Caucasus Mountains
- Persian Gulf
- Sea of Japan
- Thar Desert

Animal 117

Suggested topics:

- Javan rhinoceros
- Red-crowned crane
- Siamese fighting fish
- Siberian lynx
- White-cheeked gibbon

Tourist attraction 118

Suggested topics:

- Ben Thanh Market (Vietnam)
- Burj Khalifa (UAE)
- Five Grand Palaces (South Korea)
- Forbidden City (China)
- Hiroshima Peace Memorial (Japan)

City 119

Suggested topics:

- Abu Dhabi, UAE
- Bangkok, Thailand
- Jerusalem, Israel
- Dharamsala, India
- Novosibirsk, Russia

Cover page 120

Name _____

Physical feature

Select a physical feature of Asia. Write notes about it to complete each section.

_____
(Name of physical feature)

Location

_____
_____
_____

Interesting facts

_____
_____
_____
_____
_____
_____
_____
_____
_____
_____

Description

_____
_____
_____
_____
_____
_____
_____
_____
_____
_____

Animals or plants

_____
_____
_____
_____

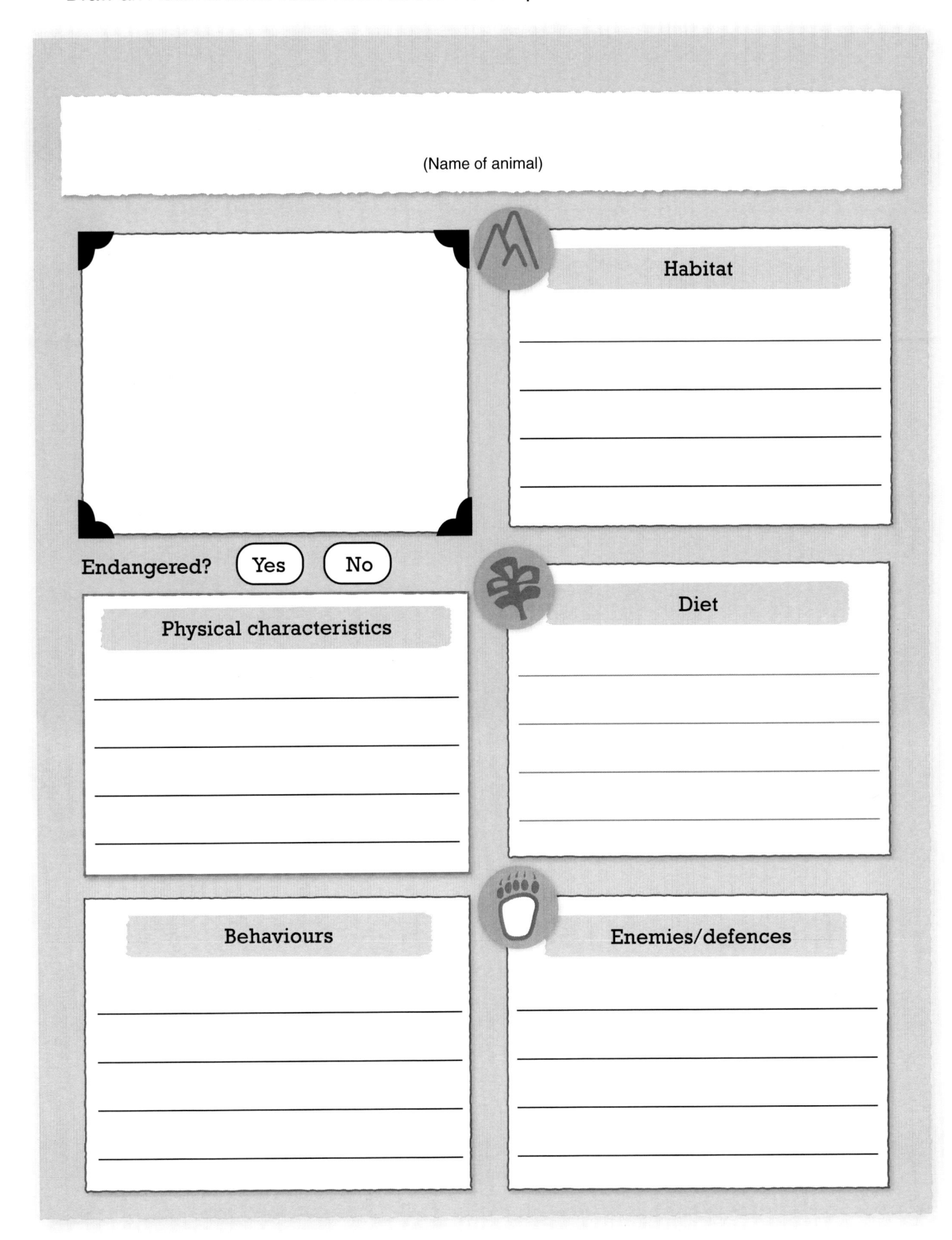

Name _____

Animal

Draw an Asian animal. Write notes about it to complete each section.

(Name of animal)

Endangered? Yes No

Physical characteristics

Habitat

Diet

Behaviours

Enemies/defences

www.prim-ed.com Prim-Ed Publishing

Exploring geography: Asia

117

Name _____

Tourist attraction

Draw an Asian tourist attraction. Then write notes about it to complete each section.

_____
(Name of tourist attraction)

Location

_____
_____
_____
_____

Description

_____
_____
_____
_____
_____
_____
_____
_____
_____
_____

Interesting facts

_____
_____
_____
_____

Name _____

City

Select an Asian city you would like to visit. Write notes about it to complete each section.

My trip to _____
(Name of city)

Location

_____
_____
_____
_____

How I would get there

_____
_____
_____
_____
_____

Things I would see and do

_____
_____
_____
_____
_____
_____
_____
_____
_____

Foods I would eat

_____
_____
_____
_____
_____

Learning the language

How to say 'hello':

_____

How to say 'goodbye':

_____

ASIA

Answers

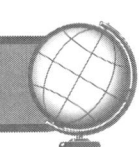

Page 7
1. both size and population
2. Europe
3. Atlantic Ocean
4. Most of Asia is located in both the Northern and Eastern hemispheres.
5. absolute location

Page 8
A. Europe, Australia, south-west, Arctic, south, Pacific
B. Pupils should colour Europe orange, use blue to circle the Pacific Ocean and draw a kangaroo next to Australia.

Page 11
A. 1. c 2. f 3. h 4. e 5. d 6. b 7. g 8. i 9. a

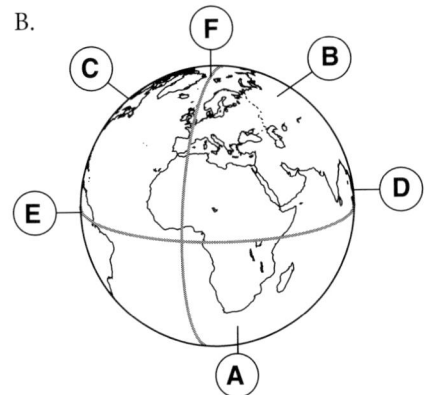

B. (globe diagram with labels A, B, C, D, E, F)

Page 13
A.
1. equator
2. prime meridian
3. north
4. 75°E
5. 90°N
6. latitude lines
7. 15 degrees
8. parallels
9. 30°N
10. meridians

B. Most places in Asia are north of the equator and east of the prime meridian.

Page 14
A. 1. No 2. Yes 3. No 4. No 5. Yes 6. No 7. Yes 8. No 9. No

B. Three: Asia, Australia and Antarctica

Page 16
Across
1. Pacific
5. Africa
6. hemispheres
7. relative
8. equator

Down
2. Asia
3. Europe
4. projection

Page 19
1. 50, 6
2. South-West Asia
3. Russia
4. Tokyo, Japan
5. Asia has 4 billion people and it is expected to grow to 5 billion by 2050.

Page 20
A. Teacher check. Answers may vary.

Page 21
B. 1. Yes 2. No 3. Yes 4. Yes 5. No 6. Yes 7. Yes 8. No 9. Yes 10. No

C. 1. 1970–1990
   2. more than 6 billion

Page 23
Pupils should colour Mongolia, South Korea, Sri Lanka, Turkey and Yemen in five different colours.

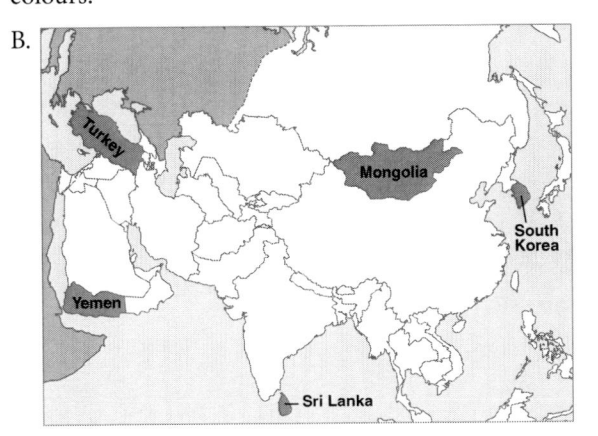

B. (map of Asia with Turkey, Mongolia, South Korea, Yemen, Sri Lanka labelled)

Page 24
A.

Rank	Country	Square kilometres
1	Russia	12 788 842
2	China	9 596 961
3	India	3 287 263
4	Kazakhstan	2 724 900
5	Saudi Arabia	2 149 690

Page 25
B. Pupils should colour Russia, China, India, Kazakhstan and Saudi Arabia in five different colours.

The five largest countries
1. Russia
2. China
3. India
4. Kazakhstan
5. Saudi Arabia

Answers

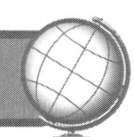

Page 27

A. 1. two   2. Iran
    3. three   4. 127 million, 253 thousand
    5. 1st: China, 10th: Myanmar
    6. Pakistan   7. 128 785 000

B. Teacher check

Page 28

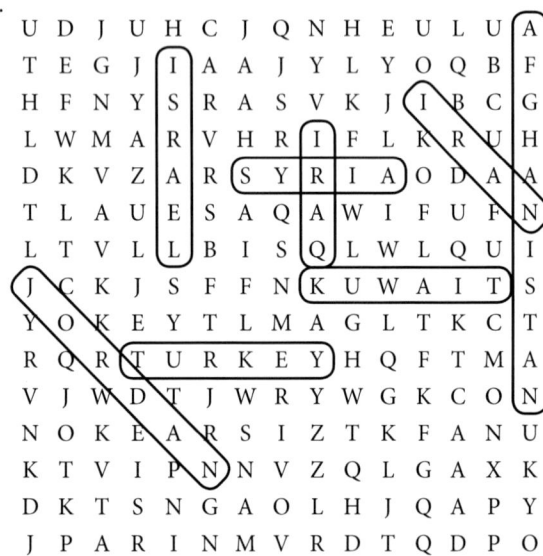

A.

```
U D J U H C J Q N H E U L U A
T E G J I A A J Y L Y O Q B F
H F N Y S R A S V K J I B C G
L W M A R V H R I F L K R U H
D K V Z A S Y R I A O D A A
T L A U E S A Q A W I F U N
L T V L L B I S Q L W L Q U I
J C K J S F N K U W A I T S
Y O K E Y T L M A G L T K C T
R Q R T U R K E Y H Q F T M A
V J W D T J W R Y W G K C O N
N O K E A R S I Z T K F A N U
K T V I P N V Z Q L G A X K
D K T S N G A O L H J Q A P Y
J P A R I N M V R D T Q D P O
```

Page 29

B. Pupils should colour the map and complete the paragraph.
Teacher check. Answers may vary.

Page 30

A. 1. countries
    2. billion
    3. India
    4. second
    5. Mumbai
    6. Maldives
    7. Bangladesh
    8. Sri Lanka

Page 31

B. Pupils should circle the Maldives in blue and colour each of the other six countries a different colour.
Teacher check. Answers may vary.

Page 32

B. 1. Kazakhstan
    2. Uzbekistan
    3. Turkmenistan
    4. Tajikistan
    5. Kyrgyzstan

Page 34

A. region, Siberia, 30, population, country, Europe, Ural, Novosibirsk

Page 35

B. Pupils should colour the map and write a paragraph. Teacher check. Answers may vary.

Page 36

A. 1. Tokyo
    2. Ulaanbaatar
    3. Seoul
    4. Japan
    5. Pyongyang

Page 37

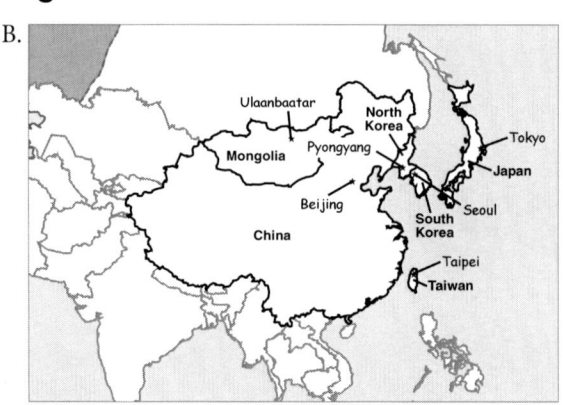

B. *Map of East Asia showing Mongolia (Ulaanbaatar), China (Beijing), North Korea (Pyongyang), South Korea (Seoul), Japan (Tokyo), and Taiwan (Taipei).*

Page 38

1. Indonesia   6. Philippines
2. Thailand   7. Brunei
3. Laos   8. Vietnam
4. Cambodia   9. Thailand
5. Singapore   10. Malaysia

Answers

Page 41

A. 1. Delhi
    2. 116 000
    3. Iran
    4. Karachi
    5. seven
    6. Chongqing
    7. more than 10 million

B. 1. 13
    2. 8 211 000
    3. Tehran and Hong Kong

Page 42

Across	Down
3. Indonesia	1. Russia
5. Mumbai	2. fifty
8. North	4. South
	6. billion
	7. China

Page 45

1. Himalayas
2. desert
3. Caribbean Sea
4. The Dead Sea is the lowest lake on the Earth
5. Yangtze, Chang Jiang

Page 46

A. 1. Gobi Desert   5. West Siberian Plain
    2. Mount Everest   6. north
    3. desert   7. Deccan Plateau
    4. Ural Mountains   8. Manchurian Plain

B. Pupils should colour the following:

   Brown: Altay Mountains, Himalaya Mountains, Ural Mountains, Zagros Mountains

   Yellow: Arabian Desert, Gobi Desert, Taklimakan Desert, Thar Desert

   Blue: Ganges River, Huang He River, Indus River, Ob River, Yangtze River, Yenisei River

   Green: Central Siberian Plateau, Deccan Plateau, Manchurian Plain, West Siberian Plain

Page 49

A. 1. No   6. Yes
    2. No   7. No
    3. Yes   8. No
    4. No   9. Yes
    5. No   10. Yes

B. 1. about 800 metres
    2. 349 metres

Page 51

A.–B.   Teacher check. Answers may vary.

Page 53

1. water   4. plates
2. continents   5. peninsula
3. geographers   6. collided

Crack the code!

Some people think the Indian subcontinent looks like an <u>arrowhead</u>.

Page 55

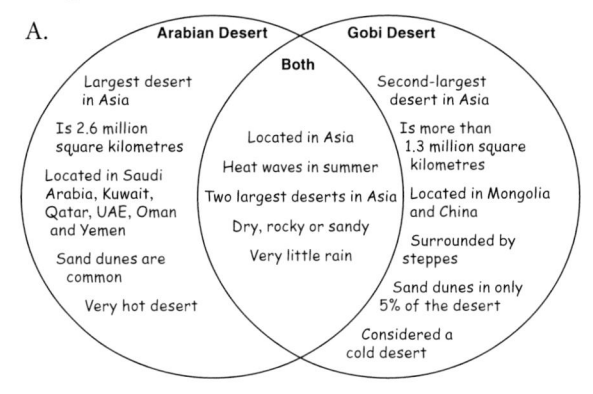

A. Venn diagram:

Arabian Desert (only): Largest desert in Asia; Is 2.6 million square kilometres; Located in Saudi Arabia, Kuwait, Qatar, UAE, Oman and Yemen; Sand dunes are common; Very hot desert

Both: Located in Asia; Heat waves in summer; Two largest deserts in Asia; Dry, rocky or sandy; Very little rain

Gobi Desert (only): Second-largest desert in Asia; Is more than 1.3 million square kilometres; Located in Mongolia and China; Surrounded by steppes; Sand dunes in only 5% of the desert; Considered a cold desert

B. 1. Saudi Arabia, Kuwait, Qatar, UAE, Oman and Yemen
    2. Mongolia and China
    3. Gobi Desert
    4. Arabian Desert
    5. Arabian Desert

Page 56

A. 1. e   2. f   3. h   4. c
    5. d   6. g   7. b   8. a

B. Teacher check. Answers may vary.

Answers

Page 59

A. 1. four
    2. mountains and hills
    3. Mount Fuji, 3776 km
    4. over 60
    5. a group of islands
    6. A series of huge, destructive waves called tsunamis can crash along the coast.

B. Teacher check. Answers may vary.

Page 61

A. 1. tropical
    2. monsoons
    3. humid
    4. tualang
    5. flower
    6. Malaysia
    7. extinction
    8. million

B. Teacher check. Answers may vary.

Page 62

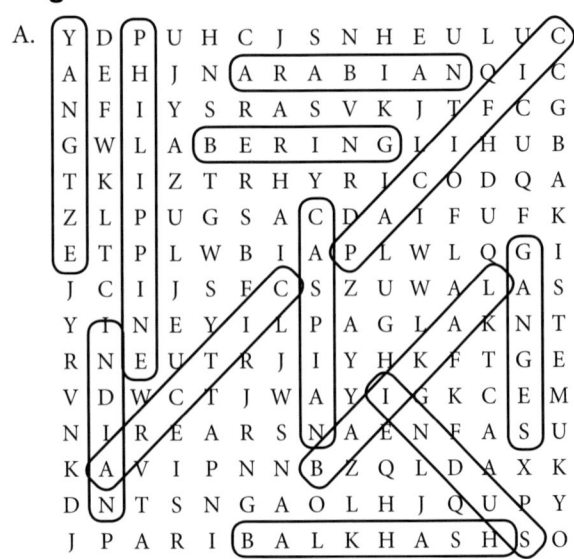

A. [word search puzzle]

B. 1.–2. Teacher check. Answers may vary.

Page 65

A. 1. Caspian Sea
    2. Dead Sea
    3. Lake Baikal
    4. Lake Balkhash
    5. Dead Sea
    6. Sea of Galilee
    7. Aral Sea
    8. Sea of Galilee
    9. Lake Baikal
    10. Aral Sea

B. 1. Russia
    2. Kazakhstan and Uzbekistan
    3. Lake Balkhash
    4. five
    5. Israel

Page 67

A. 1. Yangtze
    2. Huang He
    3. Ganges
    4. Euphrates
    5. Mekong
    6. Yenisei
    7. Ganges
    8. Huang He

B.

Rank	River	Length
1	Yangtze	6275 km
2	Huang He	5464 km
3	Mekong	4184 km
4	Yenisei	4093 km
5	Euphrates	2736 km
6	Ganges	2511 km

Page 68

Across
4. Indian
6. Siberia
7. Baikal
8. Everest

Down
1. Gobi
2. Himalayas
3. Yangtze
5. Dead

Page 71

1. China
2. The Middle East
3. rice
4. Siberian taiga
5. water buffalo

Page 73

A. 1. No
    2. No
    3. Yes
    4. Yes
    5. No
    6. Yes
    7. No
    8. Yes
    9. Yes
    10. No

B. 1. 1 590 000 000 litres
    2. $1 000 000 000
    3. about 12.5 barrels

Page 75

A. 1. resource
    2. producer
    3. energy
    4. consumed
    5. billion
    6. larger
    7. electricity
    8. carbon

B. 1. east
    2. 25 000
    3. north

Answers

Page 77

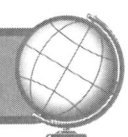

A.
```
A F B F I S D E E J R C B A Q
B I W H S H R I M P W H K T P
M S G C H N E J L O C Z J L P
C H A L E M S A M P A N S Y I
D E I Z L V A G M E O B E X O
A R W O L H B V M C T Y A H X
U M B S F L E E T I H H W B U
O E I N I M Z I T P S E T R
P N G A S F I B E U W I E G C
A I X L H K U K L N O I D Z E
X S F V T K R E L S L F E H O
P D C B W A Y F I S E K R V C
R A N W M X C O K P O N V H E
Y A T E V T U N A Z C O R S A
M V E H Z E G U L N U M X A N
```

B. Teacher check. Answers may vary.

Page 78

A. Answers will vary. Each section of the circle graph should be a different colour.

Page 79

B. 1. grain   4. rainfall
   2. per cent   5. India
   3. paddies   6. water

Crack the code!

This grass, called <u>wild rice</u>, is native to North America and is not actually rice.

Page 81

A. 1. f   2. i   3. g   4. h   5. c   6. j   7. b   8. e
   9. a   10. d

B. Teacher check. Answers may vary.

Page 85

A. 1. Orangutan   6. Birdwing butterfly
   2. Giant panda   7. Giant panda
   3. Komodo dragon   8. King cobra
   4. Rhinoceros hornbill 9. Orangutan
   5. King cobra   10. Rhinoceros hornbill

B. Teacher check. Answers may vary.

Page 87

A. [illustration of a tiger]

B. Teacher check. Answers may vary.

Page 89

A. **domesticated:** tamed
   dromedary: a camel that has one hump
   pack animal: an animal that carries large loads

B. 1. Camels carry people and large loads across long distances, just like ships.
   2. Water buffalo work as hard as machines and can plough knee-deep in mud.

C. Teacher check. Answers may vary.

Page 90

Across	Down
1. buffalo	2. fishing
5. rice	3. dragon
6. Orangutan	4. resources
8. forest	7. Tigers

Page 93

1. Japan
2. Hina Matsuri
3. Pupils go to school 240 days of the year in Japan.
4. the Great Wall
5. Asian culture is very diverse.

Page 95

A. 1. 1653
   2. It was carved into mountains.
   3. 8850 km long
   4. Angkor Wat
   5. Petra
   6. to honour his wife who died
   7. a Hindu temple
   8. more than 2000 years ago

B. Teacher check. Answers may vary.

Answers

Page 97

A.
1. Yes
2. Yes
3. No
4. No
5. Yes
6. No
7. Yes
8. Yes
9. No
10. Yes
11. No
12. No

B. Teacher check. Answers may vary.

Page 101

A.

```
A B B F I S D E E J R C B A C
B E W I S L A M B P T H K T O
M A G C B N E J L O O Z J L N
C R A L U M T N A P R A S Y F
H E I Z D V A G K E A B E X U
R H I N D U I S M A H Y I H C
I S B S H L E M T I R H R B I
S I I N I M A I J T M S T A A
T T B A S R I B N U S I A G N
I I L M K U K L I O I S Z I I
A S E R T K R E A S L F E H S
N D C U W A Y D I S E K U V M
I A G W M X U O K P O N V H E
T L T E V J U N A C O O R S A
Y V E H Z E M U S L I M X A D
```

B. Teacher check. Drawing and answers may vary.

Page 103

Teacher check. Answers may vary.

Page 105

A. 1. d 2. g 3. b 4. e 5. h 6. a 7. c 8. f

B. 1.–3. Teacher check. Answers may vary.

Page 107

Answers will vary.

Page 109

Colours will vary.

1. the emperor and empress
2. three court ladies
3. five male musicians
4. two ministers
5. three servants

Page 110

Across
2. Japan
4. Thailand
6. religions
8. culture

Down
1. calendar
3. Petra
5. Hina Matsuri
7. India

Page 112

1. Russia
2. Arabian Desert
3. Indian Ocean
4. Mumbai
5. Himalayas
6. Gobi Desert
7. Beijing
8. Yangtze River
9. Japan
10. Indonesia

Page 113

1. both size and population
2. Europe
3. Northern and Eastern
4. 50, 6
5. Russia
6. China and India
7. Himalaya Mountains
8. Arabian

Page 114

9. Atlantic
10. Russia and Saudi Arabia
11. 90
12. orangutan
13. They carry heavy loads.
14. Hinduism
15. phases of the moon
16. Angkor Wat